WATER POLLUTION
ITS IMPACT ON ENVIRONMENT AND SOCIETY

WATER POLLUTION

ITS IMPACT ON ENVIRONMENT AND SOCIETY

Edited by

Dr. Rabi Narayana Misra

M.Com., LLB., M.Phil, Ph.D.

DISCOVERY PUBLISHING HOUSE PVT. LTD.

NEW DELHI-110 002

Published by:
Namit Wasan
DISCOVERY PUBLISHING HOUSE PVT. LTD.
4383/4B, Ansari Road, Darya Ganj
New Delhi-110 002 (India)
Phone : +91-11-23279245, 43596064-65
Fax : +91-11-23253475
E-mail : discoverypublishinghouse@gmail.com
namitwasan9@gmail.com
sales@discoverypublishinggroup.com
web : www.discoverypublishinggroup.com

***First Edition:* 2016**

ISBN: 978-93-5056-790-6

Water Pollution: ***Its Impact on Environment and Society***

Preface

Water is of unique importance for life which is essential for every living beings for their survival and growth. The human body is consists of about two-thirds of water and almost every function of human body depends on it. An individual can live without food for a month, but it is just impossible to live without water for even a week. Water pollution is caused by addition of dissolved or suspended solids discharging most dangerous, harmful and toxic pollutants such as detergents, pesticides, heavy metals such as mercury, lead, chromium etc. and non-degradable bio-accumulative compounds, domestic sewages, municipality septic tank and drain water and industrial wastes. For this purpose proper management of water is highly essential, so water can be use for drinking purpose. This book is very essential for NGO's who are dealing with socio-economic development of the country. It is also helpful to the Government and other oganisations dealing on health, agriculture, industry, municipality authorities etc.

—**Dr. Rabi N. Misra**

Acknowledgements

I am thankful to all paper contributors of this book. It is not possible in my part to edit this book without their active co-operation and help.

I am also thankful to Lion Smt. Swarna Prava Misra, President of Lions Club of Brahampur Gold and all its members for conducting a National Seminar on Water Pollution Management on 24.8.2014 at Mahamayee College, Berhampur, Odisha.

I convey my thanks and express gratitudes to Mr. Tilak Wasan, the Director/Owner of Discovery Publishing House Pvt. Ltd., New Delhi for publishing this book without any hesitation. I am also thankful to his son Mr. Parul Wasan and other members of the staff of Discovery Publishing House for their kind help and co-operation in publishing the book in time.

—Dr. Rabi N. Misra

CONTENTS

Water Pollution: Its Impact on Environment and Society
Edited by: **Dr. Rabi N. Misra**
ISBN: 978-93-5056-790-6
Edition: **2016**
Published by: **Discovery Publishing House Pvt. Ltd., New Delhi (India)**

Water Pollution Management in Agricultural Sector

Manju Prava Das
Principal, P.G. Department of Rural Management, Sanjay Memorial Institute of Technology, Berhampur, Odisha

Introduction

India is a country where more than 60% of population depends upon agriculture for their livelihood. Agricultural activities that cause water pollution include confined animal facilities, grazing, plowing, pesticide spraying, irrigation, fertilizing, planting, and harvesting. The main elements of agricultural pollution are:

- Phosphates
- Nitrates
- Pesticides
- Sediment
- Faecal bacteria.

All of these reduce the quality of the water we use to drink, swim and catch fish in. Farming isn't the only cause of these problems, but it does contribute around 50-60% of nitrates, 20-30% of phosphorus and 75% of the sediment getting into our wafer sources. Agricultural pollution of surface water, groundwater and marine waters relates to the contamination of drinking water, and harmful effects on ecosystems. This paper is aimed to discuss on the ways that can minimize agricultural impacts on surface water and groundwater pollution. The various ways are:

Managing Sedimentation: Farmers can reduce erosion and sedimentation by 20 to 90 per cent by applying management measures to control the volume and flow rate of runoff water, keep the soil in place, and reduce soil transport.

Managing Confined Animal Facilities: By confining animals to areas or lots, formers can efficiently feed and maintain livestock. Discharges can be limited by storing and managing facility wastewater and runoff with an appropriate waste management system.

Managing Irrigation: Inefficient irrigation can cause water quality problems. Farmers can reduce pollution from irrigation by improving water use efficiency. Actual crop needs can be measured with a variety of equipment.

Managing Pesticides: To reduce water contamination from pesticides, people can apply Integrated Pest Management (IPM) techniques based on the specific soils, climate, pest history, and crop for a particular field. IPM helps limit pesticide use and manages necessary applications to minimize pesticide movement from the field.

Managing Livestock Grazing: To reduce the impacts of grazing on water quality, farmers can adjust grazing intensity, keep livestock out of sensitive areas, provide alternative sources of water and shade.

Meaning and Sources of Water Pollution

Water pollution is a serious problem in India as almost 70 per cent of its surface water resources and a growing percentage of its groundwater reserves are contaminated by biological, toxic, organic, and inorganic pollutants. In many cases, these sources have been rendered unsafe for human consumption as well as for other activities, such as irrigation and industrial needs. This shows that degraded water quality can contribute to water scarcity as it limits its availability for both human use and for the ecosystem.

Water pollution is a major global problem which requires ongoing evaluation and revision of water resource policy at all levels (international down to individual aquifers and wells). It has been suggested that it is the leading worldwide cause of deaths and diseases, and that it accounts for the deaths of more than 14,000 people daily. An estimated of 580 people in India die of water pollution related illness every day.

Water pollution is the contamination of water bodies (e.g. lakes, rivers, oceans, aquifers and groundwater). Water pollution occurs when pollutants are directly or indirectly discharged into water bodies without adequate treatment to remove harmful compounds.

Water is typically referred to as polluted when it is impaired by anthropogenic contaminants and either does not support a human use, such as drinking water, or undergoes a marked shift in its ability to support its constituent biotic communities, such as fish. Natural phenomena such as volcanoes, algae blooms, storms, and earthquakes also cause major changes in water quality and the ecological status of water. Water pollution affects plants and organisms living in these bodies of water. In almost all cases the effect is damaging not only to individual species and populations, but also to the natural biological communities.

Water pollution is a major environmental issue in India. The largest source of water pollution in India is untreated sewage and agricultural runoff due to which most rivers, lakes and surface water in India are polluted.

Untreated Sewage

As per a study in 2007, it is found that discharge of untreated sewage is the single most important source of pollution of surface and groundwater in India. There is a large gap between generation and treatment of domestic waste water in India. The problem is not only that India lacks sufficient treatment capacity but also that the sewage treatment plants that exist do not operate and are not maintained. The majority of the government-owned sewage treatment plants remain closed most of the time due to improper design or poor maintenance or lack of reliable electricity supply to operate the plants, together with absentee employees and poor management. The waste water generated in these areas normally percolates into the soil or evaporates. The uncollected wastes accumulate in the urban areas causing unhygienic conditions and releasing pollutants that leach into surface and groundwaters. Sewage discharged from cities, towns and some villages is the predominant cause of water pollution in India. The scientific analysis of water samples from 1995 to 2008 indicates that the organic and bacterial contamination is severe in water bodies of India. This is mainly due to discharge of domestic waste water in untreated form, mostly from the urban centres of India. Investment is needed to bridge the gap between sewage India generates and its treatment capacity of sewage per day.

Agricultural Runoff

Agricultural run-off, or the water from the fields that drains into rivers, is another major water pollutant as it contains fertilizers and pesticides. Groundwater accounts for nearly 80 per cent of the rural domestic water needs and 50 per cent of the urban water needs in India. It is generally less susceptible to contamination and pollution when compared to surface water bodies. Agricultural runoff is the flow of water that occurs when excess water from rain, melt water, or other sources flows over the earth's surface. This might occur because soil is saturated to full capacity, or because rain arrives more quickly than soil can absorb it. Surface runoff is a major eomponent of the water cycle. It is the primary agent in soil erosion by water. Runoff that occurs on surfaces before reaching a channel is also called a nonpoint source. If a nonpoint source contains man-made contaminants, or natural forms of pollution (such as rotting leaves) the runoff is called nonpoint source pollution. A land area which produces runoff that drains to a common point is called a drainage basin. When runoff flows along the ground, it can pick up soil contaminants including, but not limited to petroleum, pesticides, or fertilizers that become discharge or nonpoint source pollution.

Water Consumption in Indian Agriculture

India is one of the world's leading crop producers. Over the years, this has led to an increase in water consumption in the agricultural sector. Consumption of water for irrigation is rising. The volume of water used for irrigation in India is expected to increase by 68.5 Tr liters between 2000 and 2025.

Rice, wheat and sugarcane together constitute 90% of India's crop production and are the most water-consuming crops. Wheat, Rice and Sugarcane together constituted 91% of India's crop production (food grain and sugarcane). India has the highest water footprints among the top rice and wheat producing countries. Increase in wastewater discharge: Agriculturally based industries such as textiles, sugar and fertilizer are among the top producers of waste water. Accordingly the pollution related to agricultural sector has also risen.

Management of Water Pollution in Agricultural Sector

Water security is widely recognised as one of the major challenges to India's economic and social development. As the pollution of water is increasing due to agriculture related aspects, it has become a matter of concern to manage and control this. The various ways that can minimize agricultural impacts on surface water and ground water pollution are:

(*a*) **Managing Sedimentation:** Sedimentation occurs when wind or water runoff carries soil particles from an area, such as a farm field, and transports them to a water body, such as a stream or lake. Excessive sedimentation clouds the water, which reduces the amount of sunlight reaching aquatic plants; covers fish spawning areas and food supplies; and clogs the gills of fish. In addition, other pollutants like phosphorus, pathogens, and heavy metals are often attached to the soil particles and wind up in the water bodies with the sediment. Farmers and ranchers can reduce erosion and sedimentation by 20 to 90 per cent by applying management measures to control the volume and flow rate of runoff water, keep the soil in place, and reduce soil transport

(*b*) **Managing Confined Animal Facilities:** By confining animals to areas or lots, farmers can efficiently feed and maintain livestock. But these confined areas become major sources of animal waste. Runoff from poorly managed facilities can carry pathogens (bacteria and viruses), nutrients, and oxygen-demanding substances that contaminate shell fishing areas and other major water quality problems. Ground water can also be contaminated by seepage. Discharges can be limited by storing and managing facility wastewater and runoff with an appropriate waste management system.

(*c*) **Managing Irrigation:** Irrigation water is applied to supplement natural precipitation or to protect crops against freezing or wilting. Inefficient irrigation can cause water quality problems. In arid areas, for example, where rainwater does not carry residues deep into the soil, excessive irrigation can concentrate pesticides, nutrients, disease-carrying micro-organisms, and salts-all of which impact water quality-in the top layer of soil. Farmers can reduce NPS pollution from irrigation by improving water use efficiency. Actual crop needs can be measured with a variety of equipment.

(*d*) **Managing Pesticides:** Pesticides, herbicides, and fungicides are used to kill pests and control the growth of weeds and fungus. These chemicals can enter and contaminate water through direct application, runoff, wind transport, and atmospheric deposition. They can kill fish and wildlife, poison food sources, and destroy the habitat that animals use for protective cover. To reduce NPS contamination from pesticides, people can apply Integrated Pest Management (IPM) techniques based on the specific soils, climate, pest history, and crop for a particular field. IPM helps limit pesticide use and manages necessary applications to minimize pesticide movement from the field.

(*e*) **Managing Livestock Grazing:** Overgrazing exposes soils, increases erosion, encourages invasion by undesirable plants, destroys fish habitat, and reduces the filtration of sediment necessary for building streambanks, wet meadows, and floodplains. To reduce the impacts of grazing on water quality, farmers and ranchers can adjust grazing intensity, keep livestock out of sensitive areas, provide alternative sources of water and shade, and revegetate rangeland and pasture land.

(*f*) **Control of Water Pollution:** Excessive use of water for agriculture, industries and domestic uses is leading to water pollution, because such excess water is transformed into saline water, sewage or effluent. Unnecessary use of water must be reduced. Steps should be taken for storage of water in a proper manner.

CONCLUSION

India is a country, where more than 60% of population depends upon agriculture. As agriculture is the larger sector causing water pollution, the initiatives for management of the pollution may be effective to control the water pollution up to a greater extent. The people depending upon agriculture can be trained up in this regard to control the situation as far as possible.

Thus, proper management of water is needed. Unless it is managed in suitable manner, it causes number of problems and will ruin the human lives.

REFERENCES

ADB (Asian Development Bank) (2007), Asian Development Water Outlook 2007: Achieving Water Security for Asia, Asian Development Sank.

Briscoe, J. and R.P.S. Malik (2005), India's Water Economy: Bracing for a Turbulent Future. World Bank. Central Pollution Control Board, India, Annual Report 2008-2009, Central Pollution Control Board, Ministry of Environment & Forests, Government of India. 2009.

Central Pollution Control Board, Evaluation of Operation and Maintenance Of Sewage Treatment Plants In India-2007, Ministry of Environment & Forests. 2008.

Central Pollution Control Board, Status of Sewage Treatment in India, Ministry of Environment & Forests, Govt of India. 2005.

Colder, B and Mukherjee B (1998): Pollution Abatement Cost Function: Methodological and Estimation Issues, C.D.E., Working Paper No. 56, Delhi School of Economics, University of Delhi, Delhi

Dasgupta, A. K and Murty M. N. (1985) : Economic Evaluation of Water Pollution Abatement: A Case Study of Paper and Pulp Industry in India, Indian Economic Review, Vol. XX,No. 2, pp 232-267.

Fast Facts - Sanitation World Health Organization, 2012

National Geographic Society, Water: A Story of Hope. Washington (DC): National Geographic Society, 1995.

Water Pollution: Its Impact on Environment and Society
Edited by: **Dr. Rabi N. Misra**
ISBN: 978-93-5056-790-6
Edition: **2016**
Published by: **Discovery Publishing House Pvt. Ltd., New Delhi (India)**

Water Pollution Management

Gayatri Mandal
Asst. Prof., P.G. Centre for Management Studies,
BPUT, SMIT, Berhampur, Odisha

Introduction

Water is the greatest gift of nature. Humans have exploited this natural resource to a level where controlling water pollution is impossible. The misuse of this can cause damaging consequences and a threat to human life.

Water pollution is the contamination of water bodies (examples - Lakes, rivers, oceans, aquifers and groundwater). Water pollution occurs when pollutants are directly or indirectly discharged into water bodies without adequate treatment to remove harmful compounds. Water pollution affects plants and organism living in these bodies of water in almost all cases the effect is damaging not only to individual species and populations, but also to the natural biological communities.

The use of hazardous chemicals in manufacturing industries and agriculture cause severe water pollution as waste from these industries goes directly into nearby rivers, lakes and ponds. This not only affects the quality of water but also pose danger to several endangered aquatic species.

Some Facts on Water Pollution

- The total volume of water available on Earth is about 1.4 billion km and about 70% of the earth is covered in water.
- Fresh water in the world is only 2.5% of the total water available. Around 70% of the industrial waste is dumped into the water bodies where they pollute the usable water supply.
- At least 320 million people in China do not have access to drinking water.
- Twenty per cent of the groundwater in China is used as drinking water which is highly contaminated with carcinogenic chemicals which cause high levels of water pollution.
- Fourteen billion pounds of garbage mostly plastic, is dumped into the ocean every year.
- The nuclear crisis that occurred in Japan after 2011 Tsunami prompted Japanese government dumped 11 million liters (2 million gallons) of radioactive water into the Pacific Ocean.
- Japan created 70 km long island of dobris which is floating out into the Pacific Ocean in the 2011 Tsunami.
- The River Ganga in India is one the most polluted in the world. It contains sewage, trash, food and animal remains.
- According to the WHO (World Health Organization) and United Nations Children Emergency) Fund (UNICEF), around 2.5 billion people do not have access to improved sanitation.
- Groundwater in Bangladesh is contaminated with arsenic. Arsenic is very toxic, acute poison and a carcinogen. Approximately 85% of the total area of Bangladesh has contaminated groundwater.
- In America 40% of the rivers and 46% of the lakes are polluted and are considered unhealthy for swimming, fishing or aquatic life.

- According to UNICEF, more than 3000 children die everyday globally due to consumption of contaminated drinking water.
- On an average 250 million people worldwide succumb to diseases related to water pollution.
- Eighty per cent of the water pollution is so used due to domestic sewage like throwing garbage on open ground and water bodies. According to the survey done by Food & Water Watch cites that approximately 3.5 billion people in 2025 will face water shortage issues. This will be mainly due to water pollution. This is likely to happen because the world pollution is increasing tremendously with more water sources getting contaminated as a result of water.
- Asia has maximum numbers of polluted rivers than anywhere else in the world. Most of it contains bacteria created from human waste.
- Plastic waste being a major water pollutant is causing huge destruction of marine life and is believed to be responsible for deaths of more than 10,000 sea mammals, sea birds and various types of fishes.
- Canada has 10 most polluted rivers some of which are Petitcodiac River, Okanagan River and Eastmain River.
- Rivers in Asian subcontinent re-considered to be the most polluted. The bacteria (From human waste) found in these rivers are 3 times as much as that of the global average.
- About 1.2 billion people or 1 in 3 people in rural areas defecate in the Open defecation poses a human health risk and compromises quality in nearby water bodies.
- According to WHO and UNICEF, approximately 894 million people globally don't have access to improved water sources.
- Over 30 billion tons of urban sewage discharged into lakes, rivers and oceans each year.

- Leather and chemical industries are the major contributors of water pollution and are emerging leading market economies.
- As per UNESCO reports, 27% of the urban population do huge oil spill was caused by BP in the year 2010. Over 100 animals *i.e.* birds, turtles, mammals have been reported dead and many of them were on the endangered species list.
- Cruise ships are also a major source of water pollution They produce over 200,000 gallons of sewage which is mostly released in the ocean. Apart from that, they are also causing at least 35,000 gallons of water contamination due to oil spill.

Groundwater

Groundwater is simply water under the ground where the soil is completely filled or saturated with water. This water is also called an "aquifer". Groundwater moves underground from areas where the elevation is high, like a hilltop, to places that are lowland areas. Water movement is slow and might move anywhere from less than a millimeter up to a mile in a day. Where the watertable meets the land surface, a spring might bubble up or seep from the ground and flow into a lake, stream woodland, or the ocean. Groundwater that meets the land surface also helps keep rivers, streams lakes and wetland filled with water.

Over 50% of the United States population depends on groundwater for drinking water. Groundwater is also one of our most important sources of water for irrigation. Unfortunately, groundwater is susceptible to pollutants.

Groundwater contamination occur when man-made products such as gasoline, oil, road salts and chemicals get into the groundwater and cause it to became unsafe and unfit for human use.

Materials from the land's surface can move through the soil and end up in the groundwater for example pesticides and fertilizers can find their way into groundwater supplies over time. Road salt, toxic substances from mining sites and used motor oil also may seep into groundwater. In addition, it is possible for untreated waste from septic tanks and toxic chemicals from underground storage tanks and leaky landfills to contaminate groundwater. Drinking contaminated groundwater can have serious health effects. Diseases such as hepatitis and dysentery may be caused by contamination from septic tank waste. Poisoning may be caused by toxins that have leached into well water supplies wildlife can also be harmed by contaminated groundwater. Other long-term effects such as certain types of cancer may also result from exposure to polluted water.

Potential Sources of Groundwater Contamination

1. **Storage tanks:** May contain gasoline, oil, chemicals or other types of liquids and they can either be above or below ground. There are estimated to be over 10 million storage tanks buried in the United States and over time the tanks can corrode, crack and develop leaks. If the contaminants leak out and get into the groundwater, serious contamination can occur.
2. **Septic Systems:** On-site wastewater disposal system used by homes, offices or other buildings that are not connected to a city sewer system. Septic systems are designed to slowly drain away human waste underground at a slow, harmless rate. An improperly designed to slowly drain away human waster underground at a slow harmless rate. An improperly designed, located, constructed, or maintained septic system can leak bacteria, viruses, household chemicals, and other contaminants into the groundwater causing serious problems.
3. **Uncontrolled Hazardous Waste:** In the U.S. today, there are thought to be over 20000 known abandoned and uncontrolled hazardous waste sites and the numbers grow every year. Hazardous waste sites and the numbers grow every year. Hazardous waste sites can lead to groundwater contamination if there are barrels or other containers lying

around that are full of hazardous materials. If there is a leak, these contaminants can eventually make their way down through the soil and into the groundwater.

4. **Landfills:** Landfills are the places that our garbage is taken to be buried. Landfills are supposed to have protective bottom layer to prevent contaminants from getting into the water. However, if there is no layer or it is cracked contaminants from the landfill (car battery acid, paint household cleaners, etc.) can make their way down into the groundwater.
5. **Chemicals and Road Salts:** The widespread use of chemicals and road salts is another source of potential groundwater contamination, chemicals include products used on lawns and farm fields to kill weeds and insects and to fertilize plants, and other products used in homes and business when it rains these chemicals can seep into the ground and eventually into the water. Road salts are used in the winter time to put melt ice on roads to keep cars from sliding around. When the ice melts, the salts gets washed off the roads and eventually ends up in the water.
6. **Atmoshperic Contaminants:** Since groundwater is part of the hydrologic cycle, contaminants in other parts of the cycle, such as the atmosphere or bodies of surface water, can eventually be transferred into our groundwater supplies.

Groundwater Management

Groundwater management involves some of the most complex and socially challenging sets of issues facing India in the 21st century. Furthermore, how those issues are resolved will affect both the environment and the day to day life of most people living in rural and urban areas.

Groundwater is an invisible resource. As a result, both the dynamics of the resource basic and the services it produces are often poorly understood.

Over the past 50 year, expansion of groundwater irrigation has played a lead role in food security. Yields in areas irrigated by groundwater are often. Groundwater is a highly important source of domestic water supply. In India, roughly 80% of rural water supply for domestic uses is met from groundwater. The importance of potable drinking water is clear. As in the case of other uses, however, this is only a portion of the value of groundwater as a source of domestic supply. Wells in villages and towns free people, particularly women, from long daily walks to fetch water from springs or rivers for livestock and domestic uses. This frees time and labour for other activities. Furthermore, since water no longer has to be carried over long distances, more is often used. This can have major health benefits. In addition, because of the filtering nature of the soil and frequent long residence time underground, groundwater is commonly much cleaner than surface sources.

Groundwater is a key resource for poverty alleviation and economic development. Evidence indicates that improved water sources generate many positive externalities in the overall household micro-economy. In areas dependent on irrigated agriculture, the reliability of groundwater sources and the high crop yields generally achieved as a result often enable farmers with small landholdings to increase income. In India small and marginal farmers (those having less than 2 hectares) own 29% of the agricultural area. Their share in net area irrigated by wells is, however, 38.1% and they account for 35.3 % of the tube wells fitted with electric pump sets.

Thus, in relation to operational area, small and marginal farmers tend to have proportionally more irrigated land than larger farmers. With productivity on irrigated lands being much higher than that on non-irrigated tracts, better access to irrigation for small and marginal farmers can significantly reduce poverty.

The positive economic impact of groundwater development extends beyond well owners. Access to groundwater stabilizes the demand for associated inputs, and leads to the spread of support services for pumps and wells, creating a base for small scale rural industries. Furthermore, the spread of groundwater irrigation can increase demand for labour. In India, for example, labour accounts for approximately 44% of the cost of installing a well and the additional indirect employment created on every hectare of irrigated land through increased agricultural activity is approximately 45 days per hectare substantially higher than yields in areas irrigated from surface sources. In India for example, research indicates that yields in groundwater irrigated areas are higher by one-third to one-half than in areas irrigated from surface sources and as much as 70-80 % of India's agriculture output may be groundwater dependent.

Higher yields from groundwater irrigated areas are due, in large part, to its ease of control and reliability, Early studies indicated that water control alone can reduce the gap between potential and actual yields by about 20%. This translates into substantial benefits. Reliability is even more important. Groundwater is a key buffer against drought and normal variations in rainfall. Overall, increased yields from groundwater irrigated areas have translated into substantially higher yields and are thus is major factor in food production at the regional and national levels furthermore some of the most important food security benefits related to groundwater lie at the level of individual farmers. The vulnerability, to natural hazards of different groups in society. Including those that threaten food security, can be explained by their access to networks of key productive and social resources. For rural population, groundwater is among the most important of these recourse.

Households with access to key resources are able to build support systems that reduce their vulnerability to natural hazards. Groundwater irrigation reduces the risk that investment in labour, seed, fertilizers, pesticides and other inputs will be lost due to drought or the variability of precipitation in normal years while higher yields enable households to generate surpluses. As a result, households with access to groundwater tend to have higher levels of savings and are able to make investments in other productive resources or activities.

When drought strikes or there is a gap in rainfall these households have a dual advantage. First, they are far less likely to suffer losses than those without access to groundwater. Second, even if 'the well runs dry', households that own wells have often been able to save cash or food and invest in alternative sources of income. As a result, they have assets that can carry them through periods of scarcity or crisis.

Therefore, the expansion of groundwater irrigation has significant ripple effects, creating employment throughout rural economies.

The equity impacts of groundwater development for irrigation are, however, not all positive. Modern tubewell and drilling technology tends to be capital intensive. As a result, early exploiters of groundwater have typically been large farmers who produce surpluses for the market. Small holders growing subsistence crops often depend on supplementary groundwater irrigation using a variety of man and animal-driven water lifting devices from shallow, open wells. The expansion of energized pumping technologies tends to draw water levels down, driving shallow wells and muscle-driven devices out of business. This was, for instance, the case throughout the Genetic basin and other parts of India during the 1960s.

As water levels began to decline, some state governments in India attempted to implement administrative regulations, such as selective credit controls, restrictions on electricity connections and sitting and licensing rules. These regulations did not affect landowners who were able to install tube wells early, but limited the entry of latecomers—particularly the resource poor who depended on credit or access to subsidized electricity in order to afford the capital cost of operating and installing pumps. In addition, the economically and politically powerful were generally able to bypass regulations via 'adjustments' with officials or by depending on their own financial resources for well construction and operation.

Equity considerations are generally a major point of tension as management needs emerge. Rapid unrestricted development of groundwater has reduced poverty by giving the poor access to a key resource for production. This same pattern of unrestricted development, however, is the primary cause of over-extraction and quality problems now emerging in many parts of the world. As groundwater problems grow, marginal populations are often the first affected. Water level declines, for example, have the largest economic impact on individuals who are unable to afford deeper wells - *i.e.* the poor.

The poor are also the least well positioned to protect their interests if groundwater extraction must be reduced. Restrictions on new wells tend to affect them much more than wealthy communities where wells were installed much earlier. Wealthy individuals and communities are also often able to work around these and other types of management restrictions while poorer communities (who generally lack political as well as economic leverage) have less ability to do so. In sum, there is an inherent tension between equitable access to groundwater for all sections of society and sustainable management of the resource base.

The arrays of environmental services or values dependent on groundwater are often poorly understood. Environmental concerns related to groundwater generally focus on the impacts of pollution and quality degradation on human uses, particularly domestic supply. Development impacts on the groundwater environment are, however, different from the numerous environmental services provided by groundwater resources in their natural state.

Groundwater is an integral part of linked hydrologic, ecologic and human use systems. Changes in surface water use, groundwater use or vegetation can send ripple effects throughout these inter-linked systems—often with effects that are difficult to predict.

In India, the number of shallow tubewells doubled roughly every 3.7 years between 1951 and 1991. Rapid development has engendered its own set of issues. In many arid and hard rock zones, overdraft and associated quality problems are increasingly emerging. Although the area currently affected by groundwater overdraft may be limited, blocks classified as dark or critical increased at a continuous rate of 5.5% over the period 1984-85 to 1992-93. If continued at this rate, the number would double every 12.5 years. This implies that by the year 2017-18 (25 years from 1992-93), roughly 1532 blocks or 36% of the 4248 blocks in the listed states would be dark or critical.

Overdraft is, however, only a fraction of the management challenge associated with groundwater. Large areas, particularly in the command of surface irrigation systems suffer from water logging and associated salinity or alkalinity problems. Furthermore, development impacts on the environment and non-agricultural users can be major even where overdraft or water loggings are absent. Seasonal water-table fluctuations can affect shallow wells, low season flows in surface streams, and pollution loads. The impact of this on drinking water availability, the poor and the environment can be major.

Furthermore, it is important to recognize that overdraft and water level declines typically affect the sustainability of uses that are dependent on groundwater long before the resource base itself is threatened with physical exhaustion. Many uses and environmental values depend on the depth to water—not the volume theoretically available. In the case of the Ganges basin, for example, water level declines would exclude the poor from access to groundwater (due to the cost of increasing well depth) and would reduce base flows in streams long before the aquifer would face any threat of depletion. The Ganges basin contains, in some locations, over 20 thousand feet of saturated sediment. Dewatering of only the top few tens of feet would, however, have tremendous economic and environmental impacts.

Pollution or quality declines can cause reductions in water availability that is far less reversible than overdraft. Non-point source pollution from agriculture and other sources combined with point source pollution represents a major management challenge. Furthermore, not all quality problems are human induced. Probably the most extensive case of arsenic poisoning from groundwater is that of Bangladesh and West Bengal. Arsenic occurs naturally in the groundwaters abstracted from the alluvial deltaic sediments of the Ganges-Brahmaputra-Meghna river systems and an area around 75,000 km^2 is thought to be affected by groundwater with high arsenic concentrations.

Clearly pollution loads have increased substantially over recent decades with increases in the use of agricultural chemicals, industrial discharges and urban waste.

Many individuals, groundwater professionals included, conceptualize groundwater as flowing smoothly through the earth with rapid recharge from rainfall and relatively uniform water quality. In reality, however, complex rock formations and differential recharge rates result in far more complicated dynamics.

The amount of arsenic encountered in water from a given well can depend on the amount of organic matter available precisely where the well was drilled. A well that happens to pass near a tree trunk buried deep underground may have substantially more arsenic than a well drilled only a short distance away.

Managing uncertainty is thus a major part of any groundwater management equation.

Groundwater is an invisible, poorly understood resource, Pollution and declining water levels represent direct threats to the sustainability of environmental, domestic, agricultural and industrial uses dependent on groundwater. In addition, as demands grow and the limits of sustainable extraction become evident, competition between agricultural and other users is increasing rapidly. Each person extracts as much groundwater as possible in order to capture benefits for themselves before the resource is exhausted. The net result can be a spiral of growing demands and decreasing availability. Competition is, thus, a critical social issue that must be addressed in order to manage groundwater on a sustainable basis.

The social challenges inherent in resolving competition over groundwater resources. These are:

- **Interdependency:** Groundwater is a lynchpin that links and creates points of interdependency between agricultural, environmental and economic systems. Environmental values, access for the poor to water, food security during drought years and the economic viability of different crops may, for example, all depend on the maintenance of specific water-table or water quality conditions. These conditions are, in turn, often dependent on water use patterns. Recharge from 'inefficient' surface irrigation systems, for example, often helps to maintain high groundwater levels and, through that, base flows in rivers, groundwater access for the poor and so on.
- **The public good nature of many groundwater services:** Individual users can only capture the 'extractive' values associated with groundwater, i.e. products produced by pumping and using it in a specific application. This extractive value does not, however, reflect the environmental, drought buffer and other services produced by groundwater when it is left in the aquifer. These services *Bre public goods*- while individuals may benefit from them, the conditions depend on the cumulative actions of all users. There are strong economic incentives for individuals to over pump groundwater or ignore their contribution to pollution of an aquifer. This leads to chronic undervaluation of groundwater when it is sold in water markets or analyzed using standard economic approaches.

- **Scale:** In most cases, groundwater cannot be managed at a very local scale. Aquifers generally extend under regions encompassing anywhere from tens to thousands of villages. As a result aquifer dynamics limit the impact individuals or villages can have on groundwater conditions. At the same time, approaches to management implemented through state agencies are often difficult to adapt in ways that reflect local or regional variations in groundwater conditions and use.

In some cases groundwater rights are established that specify the volume individuals are allowed to pump, the types of uses permitted and whether or not the water can be sold to other users. Water markets are widely advocated as a mechanism for ensuring water is allocated to the highest value uses wherever transferable water rights have been established.

Approaches based on regulation and the establishment of individual water rights and water markets face tremendous challenges in India. On a purely practical level, how groundwater rights could be established, monitored and enforced given the millions of wells and conditions in rural India, is far from clear. Regulation would also be difficult and probably highly inequitable in practice. A model bill for groundwater regulation was initially circulated by the Central Groundwater Board in the early 1970s. It proposes a highly centralized system of regulation by state agencies. Modified versions of this have now been adopted in a few locations in India but little implementation has actually occurred.

Beyond the practical limitations of approaches based on individual rights and regulation by the state, however, it is important to recognize the inherently incomplete nature of approaches based on rights, regulation and water markets. It is difficult to define water rights (whether allocated to individuals or communities) in ways that capture the interdependent and public good nature of the services produced by groundwater. When rights are transferable through market mechanisms, the values reflected in the market still tend to be the direct use values rather than the public goods. When attempts are made to regulate groundwater use and transfers in ways that protect public goods approaches rapidly become complex and inflexible-unable to respond to the diverse conditions encountered at local levels or to the dynamic nature of conditions.

Because of the above limitations, approaches to groundwater management need to reflect the political nature of such decision making in order to be effective. The public good nature of groundwater services and inter-linked and often poorly understood character of systems dependent on groundwater tends to generate substantial debate over management approaches and objectives. How this competition is resolved generally depends on the ability of different groups to first understand the nature of emerging problems and management options and second to insert their views into the decision making process that determines management actions.

Under current conditions, groundwater management decisions are effectively based on economic power - the ability of individuals to afford the costs of deepening their own wells and keep on pumping. Resolving this probably requires approaches based on balance of power concepts and explicit recognition of the political nature of management needs.

Key points of leverage that may encourage the development of effective groundwater management systems could include: (*i*) improved access to information; (*ii*) legal standing for groups and individuals to force protection of public interest values; and (*iii*) the creation of management organizations capable of functioning at an intermediate scale (*i.e.* between the village and the state).

CONCLUSION

We all know that water pollution can affect our health badly and seriously. It can cause such sicknesses and diseases that will badly affect our health. We all know how important water is. Water is essential to our body. Neither we nor every living thing can't survive without water and so therefore, we should keep protect, save and help prevent our waters from being polluted. We should act as early as now, we should save rivers seas and oceans, and other bodies of water because we will also bare the burden of this problem. Let us be disciplined and responsible enough to save, protect and conserve not only sources of water but also our mother nature because our nature provides and helps us in our daily lives. Let's just realize how important our mother nature is. It is our only source of living .Let us not destroy it nor pollute it.

REFERENCES

ISET & UNDESA (1999), Groundwater and Society: Resources, Tensions & Opportunities, and Themes in Groundwater Management for the 21st Century.

Moench Marcus (1996), Groundwater Policy; Issues and Alternatives in India, International Irrigation Management Institute, IIMI Country Paper, India, No. 2, Colombo, pp. 61.

World Bank (1998), India: Water Resources Management Sector Review, Groundwater Regulation and Management Report, Washington D.C., pp. 98.

Water Pollution: Its Impact on Environment and Society
Edited by: Dr. Rabi N. Misra
ISBN: 978-93-5056-790-6
Edition: 2016
Published by: Discovery Publishing House Pvt. Ltd., New Delhi (India)

CHAPTER 3

Green Marketing
A Step to Stop Water Pollution

Ms. Akankshya Patnaik
Research Scholar
Dept. of Business Administration
(Berhampur University)

Introduction

Water the unique ingredient of life, which is essential for every living beings for their survival & growth. It is found from various research surveys that human body is consists of about two-thirds of water and almost every function of human body depends on it. It is also seen that an individual can live without food for a month, but it is just impossible to live without water for even a week. Loss of mere ten to fifteen percentage of water can kill us.

Very interestingly, it is seen that our earth the so called blue planet consists of more than 75% of water still it could able to provide less than one percentage of water suitable for human consumption. Now-a-day, it is seen that mere source of life the water is also not in a condition of drinking. In spite of that water has its magical impact. It renew and cleanse itself by allowing pollutants to settle down through segmentation or break down or by diluting the pollutants to a point; where they are not in harmful concentrations. However this process is time taking and has a saturation point of dissolving harmful concentration into it. Whereas the human needs are unlimited and to satisfy the unlimited human needs now our environment is in the lap of danger. Then the question arises here that what are the various causes behind this disaster? The answer is only one. That is we the **human.** The so called intelligent human beings are now wildly in search of name and fame. They are unaware of losing the natural gifts. As a result of which the rising pace of pollutants will pace a problem for the entire human beings and will be a threat for the future generation.

It is noticed that water pollution are basically from two sources: point sources & non-point sources. Point sources include industrial waste, septic system and other source of pollutants which directly discharge into the water resource. On the other hand the non-point sources of pollutants are very difficult to identify. It can be fertilizer and pesticides from plants, chemicals from construction sites and mines, animal waste or landfill etc.

Now-a-days various surveys and planning are undertaken by government and NGO's in order to reduce the impact of pollutants. Numbers of steps has been taken to remove the pollutants from air and water. In addition to that, various commercial organizations also take serious steps to counter the pollution problem through **Green Marketing.** This concept evolves a new method to create, communicate and promote various eco-friendly products to the customer. Not only this Green marketing concept brought a change in modifying the product, standardizing the process, brought sustainability in packing, modifying the concept of advertising and disposing the product in proper way. Thus green marketing becomes eco-friendly marketing which basically believes in 3 R's concepts Reduce, Reuse, Recycle. This article honestly conveys the concept of green marketing basing upon the essential steps taken by the various agencies to meet the challenges of water pollution. It highlights the various ways in which the impact of pollutants being faded away by the emerging of Green or ecological or environmental marketing concept into picture.

Objective

1. To Trace the reasons behind water pollution;
2. To understand the furious effect of water pollution;
3. To identify the majors taken to prevent water pollution;
4. To find out the impact of green marketing on water pollution.

REASONS BEHIND WATER POLLUTION

Illegal Garbage Dump or Domestic Sewage

Now-a-days illegal garbage dump & Domestic sewage become gigantic cause of water pollution in India. Water from our kitchen, urinal, wastewater of house, hospital, school, colleges, hotels and restaurants, etc., are dumped into sea or rivers. It is found that many developed communities water are processed or treated before dumping which reduce its harmful effect. But in many under developed areas people directly dump the waste and wastewater into available water bodies causing various harmful water born diseases to the living beings.

Agriculture Waste

Presently the fertilizers and pesticides which are basically used to decrease the effect of insects and increase the rate of growth, maintaining the production quantity, increasing the size of the product which ultimately becomes the basic cause of agricultural pollution. Those harmful fertilizers and pesticides which completely do not disappear mix with water and seeps into the ground causing soil pollution and rest is absorbed by the plant itself. Local water bodies contaminate with the ground water causing local water bodies polluted.

Industrial Waste

The present 21st century scenario is quite different from the past. The agricultural society now turns into a developed industrial belt. If we look deep into the changing circumstances we will find that lack of effective policies and poor enforcement drive allow many industries to bypass the prevailing laws made by the authorized pollution control board. As a result of which mass scale pollution affected the lives of common people. The Unplanned growth of industries becomes the main cause of industrial pollution. Inefficient waste disposal by industries become the vital cause of soil and water pollution. Industrial waste contaminates with various sources of drinking water, leaves unwanted toxins to the air and reduces the quality of the soil.

Furious Effect of Water Pollution

- It has been noticed from various research survey's that water pollution is the major source of death and disease worldwide. More than 14000 people are affected daily. It is found that more than 580 people die out of water or water related illness everyday in India.
- Around 90% of drinking water in China is polluted, as per 2007 report they don't have access to safe drinking water.
- As per the most recent national report of USA, 45 per cent of assessed stream miles. 47 per cent of assessed lake acres, and 32 per cent of assessed bays and estuarine square miles were classified as polluted.
- Due to ecological imbalance many areas even don't able to get rain regularly and depend upon others sources like water tanker and purchasing their water for even their drinking water.
- Sometimes Oxygen-depleting substances may be from plant matter (e.g. leaves and grass) or man-made chemicals. Other natural and anthropogenic substances may cause turbidity (cloudiness) which blocks light and disrupts plant growth, and blocks the gills of some fish species.
- Domestic sewage increases the content of chemical element requires for life not only this the organic human waste

serve as a food for algae and bacteria which ultimately use to over populate the organisms and decrease dissolved oxygen creating difficulties for other organization to live.

- Pollutants from Sewage cause various diseases like liver and kidney damage, Giardiasis, Amoebic dysentery and cholera.
- It is found from various researches that water-borne diseases are a major cause of morbidity and mortality.
- Crops absorb the hazardous fertilizers and pesticides which are being ultimately eaten by human beings and animals causing various diseases.
- Water comes into contact with heavy metals, harmful chemicals, radioactive waste and even organic sludge these are either dumped into sea or river which are realised into ground. As a result this ground water contaminate with the water which are directly or indirectly come in contact with animals and human beings causing harmful diseases.

Majors to Prevent Water Pollution

- Disposing off your trash in proper manner and incorporate recycling habits as far as possible. Non degradable products like polythene, paints, automobile oil, polishes, cleaning products, sanitary napkins, tampons and diapers should not be put into toilet or sink. This can further end up damaging the process of sewage treatment.
- Toxic products like chemicals, paints, automobile oil, polishes and cleaning products should be taken ample care in storing and disposing. It is mostly advised to use non-toxic products for the house as far as possible.
- Do not use colour bathing bars. They are known to contribute more to water pollution.
- If one spot litter into streams, lakes, rivers, beaches, seas or any water system, after determine that it is safe, collect them and dispose them off in any nearby waste disposal.

- Automobile oil must be used in a right way to avoid leakage of toxic fluid and it must be reused as much as possible.
- As much as possible try to use environmentally products like toiletries, soaps, cleaning materials, etc.
- Try to plant lots of trees and flowers around your home, so that when it rains, chemicals from your home do not easily drain into the water.
- Intelligently try to use that much water how much is needed and actively try to prevent running waterwaste at the time of house hold works. It not only helps to prevent water shortage but also helps to lessen the amount of water needs to be treated.
- If you use chemicals and pesticides for your garden make sure it must be used and stored properly. Try most of time to use organic manure instead of chemicals which will not only help for your plants growth and health but also helps for your health and safety.
- It is better to avoid packaged water as far as possible. The best way to carry a bottle of water per head when you step out of your house it not only eliminate your contribution to pollution related to plastic bottles but also it saves your money.

Green Marketing

Green Marketing refers to the process of selling products and/or services based on their environmental benefits. Green Marketing is nothing but a way of influencing the customer to use eco-friendly product. In the effort to stop water pollution Green Marketing plays a major role. Very interestingly it is seen as per Google Trends reports that more searchers of "Green Marketing" are from India then other countries:

Rank	Country
1	India
2	UK
3	USA
4	Thailand
5	Australia
6	Canada
7	China

Impact of Green Marketing in Reducing Water Pollution

- Replacing paper bags or cotton bags in place of Polythene bags. In many market polythene bags are exchanged for a value which shows an attempt to make customers learn to bring their own bags and stop using polythene.
- McDonald's replaced its clam shell packaging with waxed paper because of increased consumer concern relating to polystyrene production and Ozone depletion. Waxed papers are easy to dispose.
- As a result of the increased concern over driftnet fishing and the resulting death of dolphins **Tuna** manufactures changed their fishing habits. It was also a step to save aqua life.
- Xerox introduced a "high quality" recycled photocopier paper in an attempt to satisfy the demands of firms for Jess environmentally harmful products. Which basically a step to reduce water and soil pollution.
- Various firms at present try to find markets or uses for their waste materials, where one firm's waste becomes another firm's input of production. One example of this is an Australian firm who produces acidic wastewater as a by product of production and sells it to a firm involved in neutralizing base materials.
- Kansai Nerolac has worked on removing hazardous heavy metals from their paints. The hazardous heavy metals like

lead, mercury, chromium, arsenic and antimony can have adverse effects on humans. It is a step in stopping water pollution.

- Indian Oil has invested about Rs. 7,000 crore so far in green fuel projects at its refineries; ongoing projects account for a further Rs. 5,000 crore. Diesel quality improvement facilities in place at all levels. Indian Oil refineries, several green fuel projects are under implementation. The R & D Centre of Indian Oil is engaged in the formulations of eco-friendly biodegradable lube formulations.
- Wipro InfoTech was India's first company to launch environment friendly computer peripherals. For the Indian market. Wipro has launched a new range of desktops and laptops called Wipro Green ware. These products are RoHS (Restriction of Hazardous Substances) compliant thus reducing e-waste in the environment.
- Taj chain of hotel of Tata march with a new mantra of going green by creating eco-rooms which will have energy-efficient mini bars, organic bed linen and napkins made from recycled paper. There are no carpets since chemicals are used to clean those. The rooms must have CFLs or LEDs for illumination. One of the most interesting innovations has come in the form of a biogas-based power plant at Taj Green Cove in Kovalam, which uses the waste generated at the hotel to meet its cooking requirements. By which Tata not only contribute to reduce pollution but also shows a path to other hotels to promote green concept.
- Tata's new innovation Indica EV, an electric car that will run on polymer lithium ion batteries. Tata Motors plans to introduce the Indica EV in select European markets this year.

CONCLUSION

Water pollution being an alarming danger of today which will not only effect the present generation but also deprive us from golden tomorrow. It is the high time for each and every individual to be united and work towards preventing our most valuable water from being polluted. In this effort of preventing pollution government, NGO's and many other socially concern bodies have taken their steps in water safety movement. Now many schools, colleges try to aware young mass through dramas, debate, essays, dance programs and various acts related to water. Not only this, many business houses also contributed in this moment of water safety through "Green Marketing".

Green means growth, green means freshness. The Honorable prime minister has now spread the message of "Swacha Bharat Susta Bharat". The aim is to achieve the goal of clean India within 2019. Let all the Indian should join their hands to make our India **Green.**

REFERENCES

"China says water pollution so severe that cities could lack safe supplies". Chinadaily.com.cn. June 7, 2005.

"As China Roars, Pollution Reaches Deadly Extremes". The New York Times. August 26, 2007.

United States Environmental Protection Agency (EPA). Washington, DC. "The National Water Quality Inventory: Report to Congress for the 2002 Reporting Cycle—A Profile." October 2007. Fact Sheet No. EPA 841-F-07-003.

EPA. "Protecting Water Quality from Agricultural Runoff." Fact Sheet No. EPA-841-F-05-001. March 2005.

Clasen, T., Schmidt, W., Rabie, T., Roberts, I., & Cairncross, S. (2007). Interventions to improve water quality for preventing diarrhoea: Systematic review and meta-analysis, British Medical Journal. Cited November 22, 2009.

M. Pawan, S. Payal, Green Marketing in India: Emerging Opportunities & Challenges, Mishra etal./Journal of Engineering, Science and Management Education/Vol. 3, 2010/9-14.

West, Larry (March 26, 2006). "World Water Day: A Billion People Worldwide Lack Safe Drinking Water".

Pink, Daniel H. (April 19, 2006). "Investing in Tomorrow's Liquid Gold". Yahoo. Education/Vol. 3, 2010/9-14.

Water Pollution: Its Impact on Environment and Society
Edited by: **Dr. Rabi N. Misra**
ISBN: 978-93-5056-790-6
Edition: **2016**
Published by: **Discovery Publishing House Pvt. Ltd., New Delhi (India)**

Causes for Water Pollution in India

G. Chandrayya
Head, Dept. of Commerce, Government College (A), Rajahmundry

(Dr.) Prof. R.N. Misra
Professor in Management Studies, Berhampur, Odisha

Introduction

Eighty per cent of sewage in India is untreated and flows directly into the nation's rivers, polluting the main sources of drinking water, a study by an environment watchdog showed Tuesday.

Indian cities produce nearly 40,000 million litres of sewage every day and barely 20 per cent of it is treated, according to "Excreta Does Matter", a new report released by the Centre for Science and Environment (CSE).

"The untreated waste dumped into rivers seeps into groundwater, thereby creating a ticking health bomb in India," concludes the report.

Weak or non-existent enforcement of environmental laws, rapid urban development and a lack of awareness about the dangers of sewage are all blamed for water pollution.

"Untreated sewage is killing Indian rivers," the report stated.

A 2011 survey by the Central Pollution Control Board revealed only 160 out of nearly 8,000 towns had both sewerage systems and a sewage treatment plant.

Scientists who worked on the CSE report found that thousands of small factories were dumping untreated sewage into rivers and toxic waste was being mixed with fresh water.

Laboratory tests by the team revealed that almost the entire country has nitrate levels higher than the prescribed levels — a result of sewage leaching into groundwater supplies.

Environmentalists blamed the government for failing to regulate the use of water, with the country's annual consumption expected almost to double by 2050.

Thermal Power Plants

Around 25 thermal power plants have been found to be not complying with ash pond effluent limit, government today told the Lok Sabha.

Enviornment Minister Prakash Javadekar also said in a written reply in the House that there was no proposal to revise or amend existing norms for thermal power plants for air and water pollution.

He also said that there were four power plants against which complaints were recieved regarding water pollution during 2012 to 2014.

According to details furnished in the Lok Sabha, big thermal power plants like Korba, NTPC Chhattissgarh, Kolaghat Thermal Power Station, West Bengal, Tenughat Thermal Power Station in Jharkhand, Talcher of NTPC in Odisha amongst others were found to be non-compliant with ash pond effluent limit.

Coal-based thermal power plants may pollute nearby water bodies like rivers and reservoirs if adequate settling is not provided for treatment of effluent from ash ponds, the Lok Sabha was told.

Javadekar said that directions under Section 5 of Environment Protection Act, 1986 has been issued to most of these thermal power plants.

Similarly, complaints were recieved of Paricha Thermal Power Plant, Jhansi, Rihand Thermal Power plant NTPC, Wardha Thermal Power Company in Chandrapur and Busawal Thermal Power Plant in Jaigaon regarding water pollution during 2012 to 2014.

Elaborating on steps taken to control pollution from thermal power plants, Javadekar said that stricter emission limited has been prescribed for new power plants to be located in critically polluted, urban and ecologically sensitive areas.

Other measures include imposing installation of flue gas desulphurisation system for control of SO_2 emission, mandatory use of flyash so as to achieve 100 per cent flash utilisation within 5 years, mandatory use of beneficiated coal in plants located beyond 1000 kms from *pit head* amongst others.

Causes of Water Pollution in India

Water bodies *e.g.* lake, river, ocean and groundwater get contaminated due to discharge of pollutants in the water bodies without any treatment to remove harmful compounds.

Water pollution adversely affects not only aquatic plants and animals but it also affects human beings and eco-systems.

Causes of Water Pollution

Water pollution is caused due to several reasons. Here are the few major causes of water pollution:

Sewage and Wastewater: Sewage, garbage and liquid waste of households, agriculture lands and factories are discharged into lakes and rivers. These wastes contain harmful chemicals and toxins which make the water poisonous for aquatic animals and plants.

Dumping: Dumping of solid wastes and litters in water bodies causes huge problems. Litters include glass, plastic, aluminum, styrofoam etc. Different things take different amount of time to degrade in water. They affect aquatic plants and animals.

Industrial Waste: Industrial waste contains pollutants like asbestos, lead, mercury and petrochemicals which are extremely harmful to both people and environment. Industrial waste is discharged into lakes and rivers by using fresh water making the water contaminated.

Oil Pollution: Sea water gets polluted due to oil spilled from ships and tankers while traveling. The spilled oil does not dissolve in water and forms a thick sludge polluting the water.

Acid Rain: Acid rain is pollution of water caused by air pollution. When the acidic particles caused by air pollution in the atmosphere mix with water vapor, it results in acid rain.

Global Warming: Due to global warming, there is an increase in water temperature. This increase in temperature results in death of aquatic plants and animals. This also results in bleaching of coral reefs in water.

Eutrophication: Eutrophication is an increased level of nutrients in water bodies. This results in bloom of algae in water. It also depletes the oxygen in water, which negatively affects fish and other aquatic animal population.

Treating Polluted Water

It is very important to prevent the polluting of water bodies and remove existing contaminants or reducing the concentration of these contaminants so as to make it fit for desired use. Following are some of the ways of treating polluted water:

Industrial Treatment: The raw sewage is needed to be treated correctly in a water treatment plant before it can be safely released into the environment. To reduce the amount and toxicity of waste, it is passed through a number of chambers and chemical processes in water treatment plant.

Denitriflcation: Conversion of nitrates in gas is called Denitrification. It is an ecological approach to prevent leaching of nitrates in soil. It stops ground water from getting contaminated.

Ozone Wastewater Treatment: Ozone wastewater treatment method is becoming very popular. In this method, the pollutants in water are broken downby an ozone generator. Ozone oxidizes bacteria, molds, organic material and other pollutants in water.

Septic Tanks: Septic tanks are used to treat sewage at the place of location instead of treating it in any plant or sewage system. This system is used at the individual building level. The sewage is separated into solid and liquid and treated separately.

How to Save Water

It's an old adage "No water no life". We don't give much thought about using water cautiously even though it is the basis of our daily life. With the increasing scarcity of water everywhere, it has become imperative to use water as little as possible and conserve as much as we can.

We can save gallons of water in our daily life just by making some small changes in our habits and paying more attention towards our use of water. Here are few simple and easy tips to save water around the home:

Saving Water in Kitchen: Lots of water is used in the kitchen while cooking and dish-washing. You can save water in kitchen by following: Install faucets with low-flow. Wash vegetables and fruits in a tub of water instead of washing under faucet. This water can be reused for soaking dishes or watering plants. Don't use water to defrost vegetables. Use as little water as possible to boil food, and reuse the water left after boiling. Use dishwasher only when it is full. If washing dishes by hand, don't leave water running while scraping dishes and use less detergent to minimize the use of water.

If you want cool water, keep a bottle or pitcher in refrigerator instead of running tap every time.

Saving Water in Bathroom: The bathroom is one of the places where the maximum amount of water is used in a home. Lots of water can be saved in bathroom by following: Don't let the faucet on while brushing and shaving. Fix leaky faucets. Install low-flow faucet in your sinks.

Install low-flow shower head. While waiting for water to warm up, put a bucket under the shower. Take shorter showers. If using buckets, don't use more than a bucket.

Use low-flow toilets. Keep checking for leaks. Don't use the toilet to dispose of waste and tissues.

Saving Water in other Areas of the House: You can lower your water use in other areas of the house also and save water by following:

Producing energy requires large quantities of water, so by using less electricity also you save water.

Use washing machine only when it is full. Don't use the machine to dry your clothes.

Use leftover water for watering your plants. Water plants in early morning or in evening during summer.

In manufacturing a bottle of water, huge amount of water is wasted, so buy bottled water as less as possible.

While buying appliances and fixtures, choose the one which consumes less water.

Signs That Your Home's Plumbing Needs Repair: Every system in house requires regular maintenance to avoid expensive and inconvenient emergency calls for repair or replacement. Plumbing system is one life line of the house systems, since it provides you clean water to perform all the household activities. *It is very important to keep the health* *of the plumbing* ***system in good condition and prevent it from susceptible damage and aging.***

For that you need to identify the signs of damage or aging of the plumbing system and take the action promptly.

Time to Replace your Plumbing

The signs to predict if your plumbing system is having problem are as follows:

Dripping of Water from Faucets even when closed tightly: Every faucet has a rubber or composition washer which is prone to weathering with time and causes leakage. If your faucet is leaking even when you have closed it tightly, you need to replace the waster immediately to prefect the further damage to the faucet or the internal system of the faucet. To prevent the damage to the washer one should turn on and off the faucet gently.

Increase in Water Bills: This is one indication for the leakage in pipeline. Your water meter will keep on running even if all the taps in the house are closed, and this results in the increased water bill in the end of the month. This ***leakage from pipe can cause damage to your house.*** To spot the damage in the pipeline you need to see if some part of your floor is spongy or wet even if nothing has spilled on it or there is some foul smell coming from the floor or walls in a particular area. To check the damage occurred in the outdoor areas, check if some unusual plants have grown or you can spot pools of the water from nowhere. ***Roots of the trees are sometimes culprit of the damage to the pipelines.*** If you see the similar symptoms in that case contact the plumber rite away to prevent further damage.

Low Water Pressure: In case you are getting water at low pressure from your faucet, you should contact a professional plumber to evaluate your water supply system. There can be two reasons for this low pressure, one is the mineral or rust deposits in your pipe and the second one is that supply pipes might be undersized for your household plumbing system. The professional plumber will examine the water supply capacity of the main supply and for the fixtures in your house to know where the real problem lies and if you need to replace the whole piping system or a part of it.

Rust Stains: If you notice rust strains on the surface of your tubs, toilet bowls or sink, be alert as your plumbing system might be in a trouble. The plumbing system is generally of iron pipes and this might have happened due to the corrosion inside the pipe. This corrosion may lead to a big damage due to leakage if not taken seriously and might need more repair.

Slow Drains: If the drainage is slow in one particular fixture that it might be due to the localized clog, but if is happening at all the fixture than it might be the result of mineral deposits or rusting of the pipe. This clogging at all the places is quite dangerous and difficult to detect the main source, so ***only a professional plumber can locate the location of clogging*** without creating any type of damage to your house.

Water Pollution: Its Impact on Environment and Society
Edited by: Dr. Rabi N. Misra
ISBN: 978-93-5056-790-6
Edition: 2016
Published by: Discovery Publishing House Pvt. Ltd., New Delhi (India)

Impact of Water Pollution on Environment and Society

Dr. S.K. Badatya
Asst. Prof. in Finance, MBA Dept. SMIT, Ankushpur

Introduction

Water is the important natural resources which is essential for all living beings. It is essential for the existence and survival of plants and animals. We use water in various ways like drinking and other house hold activities like washing, bathing cooking, cleaning etc. It is also used for irrigation of land, generating electricity and for transport. So water is very essential for successful productivity of agriculture, drinking, industries and transport. Hence optimum development and efficient utilization of water resources great significance.

Out of total area of earth, three-forth of the surface is covered with water and one-forth is land. However, only a very small percentage i.e. 3% of it is real use to us in our daily life. Out of total water available in the earth, about 97% of water is present in seas and oceans. The remaining 3% water is present in river, ponds, lakes, streams and glaciers. These surface waters are polluted by human beings by various ways. The time is come now to control and purify the polluted water because the major cause of diseases is use of polluted water.

Orissa is having abundant water resources about 11% of total water resources of the country. As per 2001 population Census, the population of the state is about 4% of the population of the country, while the state is capacity of 11% of the water resources of the country. The per capita availability of water in the state during 2001 was 3359 cubic meter as compared to national average of 1820 cubic meter. With increasing population and industrialization, the demand for water showing an increasing with per capita availability of water will be 2218 cubic meters by 20511. Many health hazards can be overcome by supply of clean and safe drinking water as well as good sanitation facilities. These facilities are critical components of what may be called health infrastructure. In both rural and urban areas, the coverage in Odisha was higher than national averages.

Over two-thirds of Earth's surface is covered by water and less than a third is taken up by land. As Earth's population continues to grow, people are putting ever-increasing pressure on the planet's water resources. The total volume of water available on Earth is about 1.4 billion km and about 70% of the earth is covered in water. Fresh water in the world is only 2.5% of the total water available on this planet. Water pollution can be defined in many ways. Usually, it means one or more substances have built up in water to such an extent that they cause problems for animals or people. Oceans, lakes, rivers, and other inland waters can naturally clean up a certain amount of pollution by dispersing it harmlessly. Poorer water quality means **water pollution.** We know that pollution is a human problem because it is a relatively recent development in the planet's history: before the 19th century Industrial Revolution, people lived more in harmony with their immediate environment. As industrialization has spread around the globe, so the problem of pollution has spread with it. When Earth's population was much smaller, no one believed pollution would ever present a serious problem. It was once popularly believed that the oceans were far too big to pollute. Today, with around 7 billion people on the planet, it has become apparent that there are limits. Pollution is one of the signs that humans have exceeded those limits. According to UN1CEF, more than 3000 children die every day globally due to consumption of contaminated drinking water. Asia has maximum numbers of polluted rivers than anywhere else in the world. Most of it contains bacteria created from human waste. The Ganges River in India is one of the most polluted in the world. It contain sewage, trash, food and animal remains. On an average 250 million people worldwide succumb to diseases related to water pollution. 80% of the water pollution is soused due to domestic sewage like throwing garbage on open ground and water bodies. According to the survey done by Food & Water Watch cites that approximately 3.5 billion people in 2025 will face water shortage issues. This will be mainly due to water pollution. This is likely to happen because the world pollution is increasing tremendously with more water sources getting contaminated as a result of water. Water pollution almost always means that some damage has been done to an ocean, river, lake, or other water source. A 1971 United Nations report defined ocean pollution as:

> *"The introduction by man, directly or indirectly, of substances or energy into the marine environment (including estuaries) resulting in such deleterious effects as harm to living resources, hazards to human health, hindrance to marine activities, including fishing, impairment of quality for use of sea water and reduction of amenities."*

How do we know when water is polluted?

There are two main ways of measuring the quality of water. One is to take samples of the water and measure the concentrations of different chemicals that it contains. If the chemicals are dangerous or the concentrations are too great, we can regard the water as polluted. Measurements like this are known as

chemical indicators of water quality. Another way to measure water quality involves examining the fish, insects, and other invertebrates that the water will support. If many different types of creatures can live in a river, the quality is likely to be very good; if the river supports no fish life at all, the quality is obviously much poorer. Measurements like this are called **biological indicators** of water quality.

Most water pollution doesn't begin in the water itself. Take the oceans: around 80 per cent of ocean pollution enters our seas from the land. Virtually any human activity can have an effect on the quality of our water environment. When farmers fertilize the fields, the chemicals they use are gradually washed by rain into the groundwater or surface waters nearby. Sometimes the causes of water pollution are quite surprising. Chemicals released by smokestacks (chimneys) can enter the atmosphere and then fall back to earth as rain, entering seas, rivers, and lakes and causing water pollution. That's called **atmospheric deposition.** Water pollution has many different causes and this is one of the reasons why it is such a difficult problem to solve.

Major Causes of Water Pollution in India

Water bodies *e.g.* lake, river, ocean and ground water get contaminated due to discharge of pollutants in the water bodies without any treatment to remove harmful compounds. Water pollution adversely affects not only aquatic plants and animals but it also affects human beings and ecosystems. Water pollution is caused due to several reasons. Here are the few major causes of water pollution:

(*i*) **Sewage and Wastewater:** Sewage, garbage and liquid waste of households, agriculture lands and factories are discharged into lakes and rivers. These wastes contain harmful chemicals and toxins which make the water poisonous for aquatic animals and plants. With billions of people on the planet, disposing of sewage waste is a major problem. According to *2004 figures* from the World

Health Organization, some 1.1 billion people (16 per cent of the world's population) don't have access to safe drinking water, while 2.6 billion (40 per cent of the world's population) don't have proper sanitation (hygienic toilet facilities); the position hasn't improved much since. Sewage disposal affects people's immediate environments and leads to water-related illnesses such as diarrhea that kills 3-4 million children each year. (According to the World Health Organization, water-related diseases could kill 135 million people by 2020. Around half of all ocean pollution is caused by sewage and wastewater.

(*ii*) **Dumping:** Dumping of solid wastes and litters in water bodies causes huge problems. Litters include glass, plastic, aluminum, Styrofoam etc. Different things take different amount of time to degrade in water. They affect aquatic plants and animals.

(*iii*) **Industrial Waste:** Industrial waste contains pollutants like asbestos, lead, mercury and petro-chemicals which are extremely harmful to both people and environment. Each year, the world generates 400 billion tons of industrial waste, much of which is pumped untreated into rivers, oceans, and other waterways. Around 70% of the industrial waste is dumped into the water bodies where they pollute the usable water supply. Industrial waste is discharged into lakes and rivers by using fresh water making the water contaminated.

(*iv*) **Oil Pollution:** Sea water gets polluted due to oil spilled from ships and tankers while traveling. The spilled oil does not dissolve in water and forms a thick sludge polluting the water.

(*v*) **Acid Rain:** Acid rain is pollution of water caused by air pollution. When the acidic particles caused by air pollution in the atmosphere mix with water vapour, it results in acid rain. A lot of toxic pollution also enters wastewater from-highway **runoff.** Highways are typically covered with a cocktail of toxic chemicals—everything from spilled fuel and *brake* fluids to bits of worn tires (themselves made from chemical additives) and exhaust emissions. When it rains, these chemicals wash into drains and rivers. It is not unusual for heavy summer rainstorms to wash toxic chemicals into rivers in such concentrations that they kill large numbers of fish overnight.

(*vi*) **Global Warming:** Due to global warming, there is an increase in water temperature. This increase in temperature results in death of aquatic plants and animals. This also results in bleaching of coral reefs in water.

(*vii*) **Eutrophication:** Eutrophication is an increased level of nutrients in water bodies. This results in bloom of algae in water. It also depletes the oxygen in water, which negatively affects fish and other aquatic animal population. It is very important to prevent the polluting of water bodies and remove existing contaminants or reducing the concentration of these contaminants so as to make it fit for desired use. Following are some of the ways of treating polluted water.

(*viii*) **Industrial Treatment:** The raw sewage is needed to be treated correctly in a water treatment plant before it can be safely released into the environment. To reduce the amount and toxicity of waste, it is passed through a number of chambers and chemical processes in water treatment plant.

(*ix*) **Gentrification:** Conversion of nitrates in gas is called Gentrification. It is an ecological approach to prevent leaching of nitrates in soil. It stops ground water from getting contaminated.

(*x*) **Ozone Wastewater Treatment:** Ozone wastewater treatment method is becoming very popular. In this method, the pollutants in water are broken down by an ozone generator. Ozone oxidizes bacteria, molds, organic material and other pollutants in water.

(*xi*) **Septic Tanks:** Septic tanks are used to treat sewage at the place of location instead of treating it in any plant or sewage system. This system is used at the individual building level. The sewage is separated into solid and liquid and treated separately.

How to save water in your daily life?

It's an old adage *"No water no life"*. We don't give much thought about using water cautiously even though it is the basis of our daily life. With the increasing scarcity of water everywhere, it has become imperative to use water as little as possible and conserve as much as we can. We can save gallons of water in our daily life just by making some small changes in our habits and paying more attention towards our use of water. Here are few simple and easy tips to save water around the home:

(*i*) **Saving water in kitchen:** Lots of water is used in the kitchen while cooking and dish-washing. You can save water in kitchen by following:

Install faucets with low-flow. Wash vegetables and fruits in a tub of water instead of washing under faucet. This water can be reused for soaking dishes or watering plants. Don't use water to defrost vegetables. Use as little water as possible to boil food, and reuse the water left after boiling. Use dish-washer only when it is full. If washing dishes by hand, don't leave water running while scraping dishes and use less detergent to minimize the use of water. If you want cool water, keep a bottle or pitcher in refrigerator instead of running tap every time.

(*ii*) **Saving water in bathroom:** The bathroom is one of the places where the maximum amount of water is used in a home. Lots of water can be saved in bathroom by following:

Don't let the faucet on while brushing and shaving. Fix leaky faucets. Install low-flow faucet in your sinks. Install low-flow shower head. While waiting for water to warm up, put a bucket under the shower. Take shorter showers.

If using buckets, don't use more than a bucket. Use low-flow toilets. Keep checking for leaks. Don't use the toilet to dispose of waste and tissues.

(*iii*) Saving water in other areas of the house: You can lower your water use in other areas of the house also and save water by following:

Producing energy requires large quantities of water, so by using less electricity also you save water. Use washing machine only when it is full. Don't use the machine to dry your clothes. Use leftover water for watering your plants. Water plants in early morning or in evening during summer. In manufacturing a bottle of water, huge amount of water is wasted, so buy bottled water as less as possible. While buying appliances and fixtures, choose the one which consumes less water.

Effects of Water Pollution

Water covers 70% of the Earth's surface and makes up over 60% of the human body. Water pollution affects marine ecosystems, wildlife health, and human well-being. The answer to solving pollution is to make changes in our daily habits and pay more attention to the types of products we consume. The following lists display causes of water pollution and the effects it has on human health and the environment:

- Groundwater contamination from pesticides causes reproductive damage within wildlife in ecosystems.
- Sewage, fertilizer, and agricultural run-off contain organic materials that when discharged into waters, increase the growth of algae, which causes the depletion of oxygen. The low oxygen levels are not able to support most indigenous organisms in the area and therefore upset the natural ecological balance in rivers and lakes.
- Swimming in and drinking contaminated water causes skin rashes and health problems like cancer, reproductive problems, typhoid fever and stomach sickness in humans.

This is why it's very important to make sure that your water is clean and safe to drink.

- Industrial chemicals and agricultural pesticides that end up in aquatic environments can accumulate in fish that are later eaten by humans. Fish are easily poisoned with metals that are also later consumed by humans. Mercury is particularly poisonous to small children and women. Mercury has been found to interfere with the development of the nervous system in fetuses and young children.
- Ecosystems are destroyed by the rising temperature in the water, as coral reefs are affected by the bleaching effect due to warmer temperatures. Additionally, the warm water forces indigenous water species to seek cooler water in other areas, causing an ecological damaging shift of the affected area.
- Human-produced litter of items such as plastic bags and 6-pack rings can get aquatic animals caught and killed from suffocation.
- Water pollution causes flooding due to the accumulation of solid waste and soil erosion in streams and rivers.
- Oil spills in the water causes animal to die when they ingest it or encounter it. Oil does not dissolve in water so it causes suffocation in fish and birds.

How can we check water pollution?

There is no easy way to solve water pollution; if there were, it wouldn't be so much of a problem. Broadly speaking, there are three different things that can help to tackle the problem education, laws, and economics and they work together as a team:

(i) **Education**: Making people aware of the problem is the first step to solving it. In the early 1990s, when surfers in Britain grew tired of catching illnesses from water polluted with sewage, they formed a group called *Surfers Against Sewage* to force governments and water companies to clean up

their act . Greater public awareness can make a positive difference.

(ii) **Laws:** One of the biggest problems with water pollution is its transboundary nature. Many rivers cross countries, while seas span whole continents. Pollution discharged by factories in one country with poor environmental standards can cause problems in neighbouring nations, even when they have tougher laws and higher standards. Environmental laws can make it tougher for people to pollute, but to be really effective they have to operate across national and international borders. This is why we have international laws governing the oceans.

(iii) **Economics:** Most environmental experts agree that the best way to tackle pollution is through something called the **polluter pays principle.** This means that whoever causes pollution should have to pay to clean it up, one way or another. Polluter pays can operate in all kinds of ways. It could mean that tanker owners should have to take out insurance that covers the cost of oil spill cleanups ultimately, the polluter pays principle is designed to deter people from polluting by making it less expensive for them to behave in an environmentally responsible way.

(iv) **Our clean future**: Life is ultimately about choices—and so is pollution. We can live with sewage-strewn beaches, dead rivers, and fish that are too poisonous to eat. Or we can work together to keep the environment clean so the plants, animals, and people who depend on it remain healthy. We can take individual action to help reduce water pollution. We can take community action too, by helping out on beach cleans or litter picks to keep our rivers and seas that little bit cleaner. And we can take action as countries and continents to pass laws that will make pollution harder and the world less polluted. Working together, we can make pollution less of a problem—and the world a better place.

CONCLUSION

Water is essential for the existence of all life forms. In addition to household uses, water is vital for agriculture, industry, fishery and tourism etc. Increasing population, urbanization and industrialization has led to the decreased availability of water. We may be aware of at least some health hazards and harmful effects of water pollution. We all know that water pollution can affect our health badly and seriously. It can cause such sicknesses and diseases that will badly affect our health. Neither, we nor every living thing can't survive without water and so therefore, we should keep protect, save and help to our water from being polluted. We should act as early as now; we should save rivers seas and oceans, and other bodies of water because we will also bear the burden of this problem. It is important to utilize a good quality and unpolluted water. Let us be disciplined and responsible enough to save, protect and conserve not only sources of water but also our mother nature because our nature provides and helps us in our daily lives. Let's just realize how important our mother nature is. It is our only source of living. Let us not destroy it nor pollute it.

REFERENCE

Azeem Abdul, " Cause Effects and Solution of Water Pollution".

International Irrigation Management Institute, IIMI Country Paper, India, No. 2, Colombo, pp. 61.

Mahapatro, Ananta Prasad & Acharya, Pramath Nath: " Management of Water Resources: Problems and Prospects", The Orissa Journal of Commerce, vol. 34, July, 2013.

Prakash Dr. Satya, "Water Pollution" Chemistry Book, NIOS, NOIDA, No.3.

Sahu Rjen Kumar, "Natural Resources Management in Odisha", The Orissa Journal of Commerce, vol. 34, July'2013

The Economic Survey Odisha - 2010-11.

www.academia.edu

www.greengordo.com

Water Pollution: Its Impact on Environment and Society
Edited by: **Dr. Rabi N. Misra**
ISBN: 978-93-5056-790-6
Edition: **2016**
Published by: **Discovery Publishing House Pvt. Ltd., New Delhi (India)**

Tank Water Pollution and Health Hazards

Prof. R.P. Sarma
Director, Institute of Economic Studies,
J.P. Nagar, Bramhapur-760010

Introduction

There are two source of pollution that affects all the living beings including human beings. They are water pollution and air pollution. Water and air are the two most important ones that keep the life in living condition. If air is polluted, immediately affects the lungs, damages it and makes life short. Similarly, human beings and all living beings cannot live without water, if they take polluted water it damages the body slowly and results in death.

There are two source of pollution effect water. They are point-source and non-point-source.

Point-Source Pollution

Point-source pollution is pollution that can be traced to a definite point at which it enters the environment. Point-source pollution can come from industries that dump wastes, chemicals, or heavy metals into the environment. Toxic waste dumps and waste water treatment plants are also point-source pollution sites.

Non-Point-Source Pollution

Non-point-source pollution is more difficult to identify because it doesn't enter the water at a definite, easy-to-locate place. Often, it's caused by herbicides, pesticides, and fertilizers that eventually enter a waterway and harm the food chain.

Water pollution causes due to the introduction of chemical, biological and all sort of physical matter into large bodies of water that degrade the quality of life. One can blame fertilizers, pesticides, or petroleum derivatives for water pollution. In addition to that the other contributors towards water pollution are waste treatment facilities, mining activities, pesticides, herbicides and fertilizers, oil spills, activity refineries, failing septic systems, factories, oil and antifreeze leaking from cars, animal waste, soap from washing of car, house hold chemicals and many-more to count. Clean, pure water may be our most precious resource. Pollution is anything that spoils its cleanliness, purity, and overall quality. Many things that reduce the quality of the water pollute our ponds, lakes, streams, rivers, ground water, and oceans.

Urban Water Pollution

Pollution problems may differ depending on where one lives. In the north-eastern U.S., acid rain may be the biggest threat to fish and other wildlife. Along Lake Superior, asbestos particles from mining waste have been a problem. Timber harvest in mountainous areas can cause erosion and sediment to flow into lakes and streams. Mercury is a concern in many lakes in Wisconsin and Minnesota. Around much of the Great Lakes, PCBs and other chemicals are a concern. In most large urban communities, the main cause of water pollution is a combination of sewage and industrial waste. Unfortunately, some water can't be used because it is too polluted by chemicals of industrial waste. Eight billion gallons of fresh water flow past the city of New York every day as the Hudson River empties into the Atlantic Ocean. That's enough water to supply each of

40 million people with 200 gallons a day if it could be used. The Hudson River, however, is too polluted to be used as a water supply.

A Global Problem

Water pollution is a major global problem which requires ongoing evaluation and revision of water resource policy at all levels. It has been suggested that it is the leading worldwide cause of deaths and diseases, and that it accounts for the deaths of more than 14,000 people daily. An estimated of 580 people in India die of water pollution related illness every day. Around 90 per cent of the water in the cities of China is polluted and as of 2007, half a billion Chinese had no access to safe drinking water. In addition to the acute problems of water pollution in developing countries, developed countries continue to struggle also with pollution problems. In the most recent national report on water quality in the United States, 45 per cent of assessed stream miles, 47 per cent of assessed lake acres, and 32 per cent of assessed bays and estuarine square miles were classified as polluted.

The head of China's national development agency in 2007 said l/4th of the length of China's seven main rivers were so poisoned the water harmed the skin of those who used it. Water is typically referred to as polluted when it is impaired by anthropogenic contaminants and either does not support a human use, such as drinking water, or undergoes a marked shift in its ability to support its constituent biotic communities, such as fish. Natural phenomena such as volcanoes, algae blooms, storms, and earthquakes also cause major changes in water quality and the ecological status of water.

There is risk always in using water for drinking. The highest risk to health is the use of surface water such as tanks, streams and rivers act. Then there is less risk in shallow ground water. The lowest rick (as shown in Fig. 1) is in the mains water supply in the urban areas.

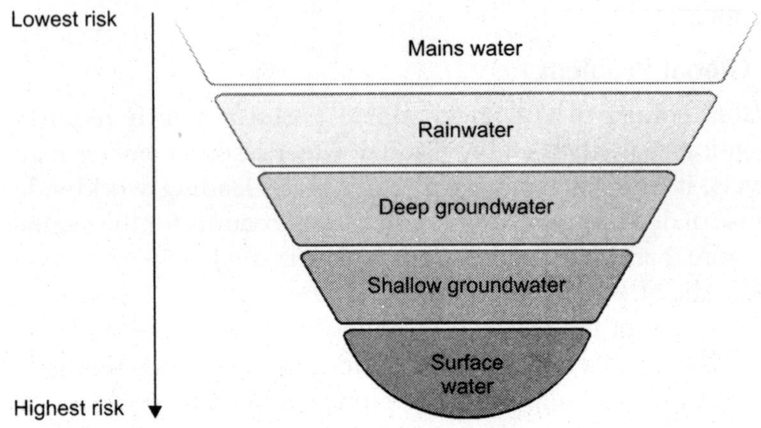

Fig. 1 : Highest to lowest risk in five types of water sources.

How Drinking Water is Contaminated

Water supply is contaminated by a variety of things:

1. Animal feces such as bird or possum droppings on the roof or from farm run-off into rivers and creeks.
2. Human feces—leaking from septic systems or wastewater drainage.
3. Pesticides - in run-off from farms or blown on to roofs.
4. Arsenic and heavy metals - in soil from old industrial and mining sites or in some bore water supplies,
5. Dust - containing chemicals blown on to your roof.
6. Air pollution - run-off from roofs in urban and industrial areas that may contain chemicals.
7. Lead - from old paint or flashing on roofs that can flake and end up in tanks.
8. Algae - including toxic blue-green algae (cyanobacteria), which are not destroyed by boiling or disinfection.
9. Nitrates - in some bore water supplies are particularly dangerous to babies.

10. Ash and debris - bushfires produce large amounts of smoke and ash, which can contaminate your water supply
11. Fire retardants - chemicals used to slow the spread of fire can contaminate water with ammonia and sulphate, making it unsuitable for humans and animals to drink.

Ground and Surface Water

Interactions between groundwater and surface water are complex. Consequently, groundwater pollution, sometimes referred to as groundwater contamination, is not as easily classified as surface water pollution. By its very nature, groundwater aquifers are susceptible to contamination from sources that may not directly affect surface water bodies, and the distinction of point vs. non-point source may be irrelevant. A spill or ongoing releases of chemical or radionuclide contaminants into soil (located away from a surface water body) may not create point source or non-point source pollution, but can contaminate the aquifer below, defined as a toxin plume. The movement of the plume, called a plume front, may be analyzed through a hydrological transport model or groundwater model. Analysis of groundwater contamination may focus on the soil characteristics and site geology, hydrogeology, hydrology, and the nature of the contaminants.

Causes Contamination

The specific contaminants leading to pollution in water include a wide spectrum of chemicals, pathogens, and physical changes such as elevated temperature and discolouration. While many of the chemicals and substances that are regulated may be naturally occurring (calcium, sodium, iron, manganese, etc.) the concentration is often the key in determining what is a natural component of water, and what is a contaminant. High concentrations of naturally occurring substances can have negative impacts on aquatic flora and fauna.

Oxygen-depleting substances may be natural materials, such as plant matter (e.g. leaves and grass) as well as man-made chemicals. Other natural and anthropogenic substances may cause turbidity which blocks light and disrupts plant growth, and clogs the gills of some fish species. Many of the chemical substances are toxic. Pathogens can produce waterborne diseases in either human or animal hosts. Alteration of water's physical chemistry includes acidity (change in pH), electrical conductivity, temperature, and eutrophication. Eutrophication is an increase in the concentration of chemical nutrients in an ecosystem to an extent that increases in the primary productivity of the ecosystem. Depending on the degree of eutrophication, subsequent negative environmental effects such as anoxia (oxygen depletion) and severe reductions in water quality may occur, affecting fish and other animal populations.

Pathogens

Disease-causing micro-organisms are referred to as pathogens. Although the vast majority of bacteria are harmless or beneficial, a few pathogenic bacteria can cause disease. Coliform bacteria are a commonly used bacterial indicator of water pollution, although not an actual cause of disease. Other micro-organisms sometimes found in surface waters which have caused human health problems include:

- Burkholderia pseudomallei
- Cryptosporidium parvum
- Giardia lamblia
- Salmonella
- Novovirus and other viruses
- Parasitic worms (helminths).

High levels of pathogens may result from inadequately treated sewage discharges. This can be caused by a sewage plant designed with less than secondary treatment. In developed countries, older cities with aging infrastructure may have leaky sewage collection systems (pipes, pumps, valves), which can cause sanitary sewer overflows. Some cities also have combined sewers, which may discharge untreated sewage during rain storms.

Organic Water Pollutants

- Detergents,
- Disinfection by-products found in chemically disinfected drinking water, such as chloroform,
- Food processing waste, which can include oxygen-demanding substances, fats and grease,
- Insecticides and herbicides, a huge range of organohalides and other chemical compounds,
- Petroleum hydrocarbons, including fuels (gasoline, diesel fuel, jet fuels, and fuel oil) and lubricants (motor oil), and fuel combustion by-products, from storm water runoff,
- Tree and bush debris from logging operations,
- Volatile Organic Compounds (VOCs), such as industrial solvents, from improper storage,
- Chlorinated solvents, which are dense non-aqueous phase liquids (DNAPLs), may fall to the bottom of reservoirs, since they don't mix well with water and are denser:
  - Polychlorinated biphenyl (PCBs),
  - Trichloroethylene.
- Perchlorate,
- Various chemical compounds found in personal hygiene and cosmetic products,
- Drug pollution involving pharmaceutical drugs and their metabolites Play media.

Inorganic Water Pollutants

- Acidity caused by industrial discharges (especially sulfur dioxide from power plants),
- Ammonia from food processing waste,
- Chemical waste, as industrial by-products,
- Fertilizers containing nutrients—nitrates and phosphates—which are found in storm water run-off from agriculture, as well as commercial and residential use,

- Heavy metals from motor vehicles (via urban storm water run-off) and acid mine drainage,
- Silt (sediment) in run-off from construction sites, logging, slash and burn practices or land clearing sites.

Macroscopic Pollution

The large visible items polluting the water may be termed as "floatables" in an urban storm water context, or marine debris when found on the open seas, and can include such items as:

- Trash or garbage (*e.g.* paper, plastic, or food waste) discarded by people on the ground, alongwith accidental or intentional dumping of rubbish, that are washed by rainfall into storm drains and eventually discharged into surface waters,
- Nurdles, small ubiquitous waterborne plastic pellets,
- Shipwrecks, large derelict ships.

Thermal Pollution

Thermal pollution is the rise or fall in the temperature of a natural body of water caused by human influence. Thermal pollution, unlike chemical pollution, results in a change in the physical properties of water. A common cause of thermal pollution is the use of water as a coolant by power plants and industrial manufacturers. Elevated water temperatures decreases oxygen levels, which can kill fish, and can alter food chain composition, reduce species biodiversity, and foster invasion by new thermo-philic species. Urban run-off may also elevate temperature in surface waters. Thermal pollution can also be caused by the release of very cold water from the base of reservoirs into warmer rivers.

According to the U.S. Environmental Protection Agency (EPA,) the average American uses between 140 to 160 gallons of water per day. Though the Earth is made up of primarily of water, only 2.8 per cent of this water is fit for consumption. The more the Earth's population grows, the more important it is to fight both against water pollution and for water conservation, to ensure that future generations have enough fresh, clean water to consume.

Prevention of Water Pollution

1. **Proper Waste Disposal:** Be diligent about where you discard hazardous waste. Don't pour paint, chemicals, oil or other hazardous material down the drain, where it will ultimately end up in the water supply. Call your waste management agency or local department of sanitation to find out where you can properly dispose of these materials.
2. **Adoption of "Go Green" Policy**: Rather than worrying about how to dispose of hazardous material, be conscientious of the products you buy to clean your home. Buy non-toxic household products whenever you can. Also use natural fertilizers like compost for your lawn maintenance.

Seven Tips for Prevention

1. **Don't Litter**: Litter casually tossed on land can end up in storm drains, ditches and streams, polluting the water. Use ashtrays for cigarettes as opposed to tossing them out the window, and put your garbage in a proper waste container rather than tossing it indiscriminately into yards, parking lots or gutters.
2. **Check Your Septic Tank**: Regularly clean your septic tank every three to five years, and pump as needed. Any untreated wastewater from a leaking septic tank can pollute any nearby streams and bays, not to mention freshwater drinking sources.
3. **Pick Up After Your Pet**: Not only does pet waste transmit disease, it contributes to water pollution when left to run off into storm drains and into waterways, beaches and bays'. In Kitsap County, Washington, pet waste contributed to the pollution that shut down some of the

shell fish beds in that area. Always scoop, double bag and dispose of waste into the garbage.

4. **Proper Car Maintenance**: If you wash your car at home, go as "green" as possible. Turn off water between rinses and wash the car with nontoxic cleansers on grass or gravel. If you change your oil yourself, recycle motor oil as opposed to dumping it. Just one quart of motor oil allowed to seep into the ground can contaminate 250,000 gallons of drinking water. If any should spill, absorb it with kitty litter and sweep up with a broom to dispose of it properly.
5. **Use More Elbow Grease**: Rather than use water to hose down your sidewalk, porches and driveways, sweep any leaves, dirt or debris with a broom. Likewise, instead of using chemicals to kill off weeds, pull them manually or use natural things like apple cider vinegar to kill things like moss on driveways or sidewalks.
6. **Change Detergents**: High phosphate levels in the water supply like lakes and streams can kill fish and wildlife. Since everyone lives in a watershed where these types of contaminants can wind up in the water supply, you can do your part keeping these levels low by changing your laundry or dishwasher detergents to low or non-phosphate detergents.
7. **Conserve Water**: Nearly three-fourths of the water you use in your home winds up flushed down the toilet or washed down the shower drain, so being mindful of how much water you actually consume helps prevent water pollution. Use a filled water jug in your toilet tank to cut down on water wasted from each flush of your toilet, and use water-efficient plumbing fixtures.

Diseases from Polluted Water

Water-borne diseases are infectious diseases spread primarily through contaminated water. Though these diseases are spread either directly or through flies or filth, water is the chief medium for spread of these diseases and hence they are termed as water-borne diseases. Most intestinal diseases are infectious and are transmitted through faecal waste. Pathogens - which include virus, bacteria, protozoa, and parasitic worms - are disease-producing agents found in the faeces of infected persons. These diseases are more prevalent in areas with poor sanitary conditions. These pathogens travel through water sources and interfuses directly through persons handling food and water. Since these diseases are highly infectious, extreme care and hygiene should be maintained by people looking after an infected patient. Hepatitis, cholera, dysentery, and typhoid are the more common water-borne diseases that affect large populations in the tropical regions. Exposure to polluted water can cause diarrhea, skin irritation, respiratory problems, and other diseases, depending on the pollutant that is in the water body. Stagnant water and other untreated water provide a habitat for the mosquito and a host of other parasites and insects that cause a large number of diseases especially in the tropical regions. Among these, malaria is undoubtedly the most widely distributed and causes most damage to human health. The important diseases that cause to humans are briefly stated in a tabular form in Table 1 below:

Table 1

Cause	Water-borne diseases
Bacterial infections	Typhoid, Cholera, Paratyphoid fever, Bacillary dysentery
Viral infections	Infectious Hepatitis Poliomyelitis
Protozoan infections	Amoebic dysentery

CONCLUSION

With the fast growth of population in the world and availability of fresh water becoming scarce, in coming years the fresh water availability would be a major crisis for human living. Unless preventive actions are taken to control pollution of water the crisis may be more difficult to tackle in future.

REFERENCES

C. Michael Hogan (2010). "Water Pollution.". Encyclopedia of Earth. Topic ed. Mark McGinley; ed. in chief C. Cleveland. National Council on Science and the Environment, Washington, DC.

Goel, P.K. (2006). Water Pollution - Causes, Effects and Control. New Delhi: New Age International, p, 179. ISBN 978-81 -224-1839-2.

Newton, David (2008). Chemistry of the Environment. Checkmark Books. ISBN 0-8160-7747-9.

Pink, Daniel H. (2006). "Investing in Tomorrow's Liquid Gold". Yahoo.

Richard Wachman (2007). "Water becomes the new oil as world runs dry".

The New York Times. "As China Roars, Pollution Reaches Deadly Extremes". August 26, 2007.

United States Environmental Protection Agency (EPA). Washington, DC. "The National Water Quality Inventory: Report to Congress for the 2002 Reporting Cycle - A Profile." (October 2007). Fact Sheet No. EPA 841-F-07-003.

West, Larry (2006). "World Water Day: A Billion People Worldwide Lack Safe Drinking Water". About.

Water Pollution: Its Impact on Environment and Society
Edited by: **Dr. Rabi N. Misra**
ISBN: 978-93-5056-790-6
Edition: **2016**
Published by: **Discovery Publishing House Pvt. Ltd., New Delhi (India)**

CHAPTER 7

Causes and Effects of Water Pollution Plagues Indian Cities

P. Subrahmanyam
Lecturer in Commerce, Government College (A), Rajahmundry

(Dr.) Prof. R.N. Misra
Prof. in Management Studies, Berhampur, Odisha

Introduction

Outdoor air pollution caused 6.2 premature deaths in India in 2010, which is a six-fold jump from the 1 lakh deaths in 2000. This makes polluted outdoor air the largest killer in India after high blood pressure, indoor air pollution (mainly from smoking chullahs), tobacco use, and poor nutrition, says the Global Burden of Disease 2013, which tracks deaths and illnesses from all causes every 10 years.

One in three people in India live in critically-polluted areas that have noxious levels of nitrogen dioxide (NO2), sulphur dioxide (SO2) and lung-clogging particulate matter larger than 10 micron (PM30) in size. Of the 180 cities monitored by India's Central Pollution Control Board in 2012, only two — Malapuram and Pathanamthitta in Kerala — meet the criteria of low air pollution (50% below the standard).

Driven Breathless

Vehicles are the biggest air polluters. "In Delhi, for example, 1,400 vehicles are added to the roads each day and contribute to more than 70% of air pollution. Barely 20 Indian cities follow Euro4 emission standards for new vehicles, most follow Euro3. Euro4 is seven years behind European standards and Euro3 is behind by 12 years," says Anumita Roychowdhury, research and advocacy, Centre for Science and Environment (CSE). In Delhi, one death takes place every hour due to air pollution.

Though air quality monitoring has doubled between 2005 and 2010 from 96 to 180 cities, the number of cities with low pollution has fallen from 10 to 2, while critically-polluted cities have risen from 49 to 89.

For indoor pollution, the daily permissible limit is 100 microgram per cubic metre (μ/m^3) for PM10 and 60 $\mu g/m^3$ for PM2.5. In many rural homes, the level is between 500 and 600 $\mu g/m^3$. "We need clean-burning chullahs, especially LPG-based ones as even kerosene burning results in toxic byproducts," she adds.

Water Woes

No one quite recalls exactly when the non-perennial natural drain across Ludhiana called Budha Dariya (river) came to be called Budha Nullah (drain), but most people who live along its banks vouch for its toxicity. So choked is the drain with industrial effluents and sewage that calcium, magnesium, fluoride, mercury, beta-endosulphan and heptachlor pesticide make both ground and tap water unfit for drinking, found a study by the Post Graduate Institute of Medical Education and Research (PGIMER) in 2008.

Compared to the other 65 wards in Ludhiana, 1.2 lakh people living in the 10 wards along Budha Nullah have much higher incidence of chronic stomach disorders, hepatitis A and cancers of the bladder, kidneys, lung, skin, colon and liver. Rickshaw-puller Sunder Lal, 50, died in October this year after battling liver cancer for two years. His wife Rano blames it on the water.

"Water is a major problem in our neighbourhood (Street-2 Gandhi Nagar) and has claimed many lives," laments Rano. Agrees her neighbour Darshan, who was recently hospitalized for two months for hepatitis treatment: "The doctors asked me to move home or get a reverse-osmosis water filter, but I can't afford to do either," he said.

Pesticides, heavy metals and antibiotics leeching into the water table also find their way into our bodies through farm produce, poultry and dairy products. In the absence of Maximum Residual Limit for several crops, pesticide residues can go through the roof. "Guidelines for pesticides in farming are not stringent and many farmers don't even know the maximum limits, they use pesticides at will to protect their crop," says Amit Khurana, food safety and toxins, CSE. Most of these chemicals are neurotoxic and carcinogenic.

Smart Samaritans

There are some trying to stem the toxic assault. All through July this year, Chandra Bhushan Tiwari, 43, gave away 11,000 saplings to people Lucknow, saying "Take 'her' (sapling) with you. She is my daughter getting wedded into your home. Take care of her, because she cares for people from birth to cremation."

Tiwari has been distributing and planting saplings every monsoons since 2006. He is close to his target of planting 1 lakh trees in his lifetime, having already planted over 85,000. "I think, now when I am almost ready to attain the target, I can push it further up", says Tiwari, a former Central School teacher, who chucked his job to take up his tree crusade full time.

VK Bharadwaj, 55, took to cycling on the busy roads of Mumbai in November 2010 for three reasons. He had crossed the age of 50 and didn't want to be what he describes as a "low hanging fruit" for doctors, he wanted to reduce his dependence on fossil fuels, and lower expenses. "The coal crisis got me to think of wanting to reduce my carbon footprint which in turn will reduce my fuel expenses," said Bharadwaj. "I bought a cycle for ₹ 30,000. That amounts to ₹ 1/km over three years as against ₹ 10/km had I used the car." And he doesn't need to stop for refuelling.

Story by Pankaj Jaiswal in Lucknow and Snehal Rebello in Mumbai

Keeping track of all the toxins that creep into our bodies through air, food and water is near impossible, but here's a list of ones that should be avoided as much as possible.

Breathing Hard

From Vehicular emissions, indoor air pollution, industry.

Carbon Monoxide: From Motor vehicle exhaust, kerosene or wood burning stoves.

Hazard: Headaches, reduced alertness, heart attack, impaired foetal development.

Sulfur Dioxide: From Coal-fired power plants, petroleum refineries, manufacture of sulfuric acid and smelting of ores containing sulfur Hazard; Eye irritation, wheezing, chest tightness, shortness of breath, lung damage.

Nitrogen Dioxide: From vehicules, electric utilities, and other sources of burning fuel Hazard; Rrespiratory infections, cough, chest pain, difficulty breathing.

Ozone: From vehicular exhaust and fumes. Hazard; Eye and throat irritation, cough, respiratory problems, asthma, lung damage.

Particulate Matter: Diesel engines, power plants, industries, windblown dust, construction dust, wood and coal burning. Hazard: Eye irritation, asthma, lung damage, heavy-metal poisoning, heart problems.

Lead: From metal refineries, lead smelters, battery manufacturing, paint. Hazard: Anaemia, high BP, brain and kidney damage, neurological disorders, cancers.

Mercury; From fossil fuels such as coal, natural gas; industrial boilers and geysers, metal refineries and cement manufacturing. Hazard: Neurological damage, extreme mood swings, insomnia, headaches, cognitive decline and, in extreme cases, kidney damage and respiratory failure.

Water Contamination

Ground and surface (rivers, lakes, ponds).

From Industrial effluents, pesticides, micro-organisms.

Agriculture: From pesticides/insecticides. Organochlorines that contain carbon, chlorine and hydrogen such as DOT, heptachlor, aldrin, endosulfan etc., and organophosphates that were promoted as less toxic by the industry such as parathion, malathion. Hazard: Reproductive system dysfunction, birth defects. Known neurotoxins that damage nerve cells, immunity, kidneys and gene structure.

Untreated sewage: From sewage, food waste and detergents. E. coli and faecal streptococci and nitrates in untreated sewage, fertilisers and manure; arsenic leeching from rock into groundwater due to over-extraction. Hazard: Water-borne diseases such as diarrhoea, dysentery, jaundice, cholera, typhoid.

Industrial Effluents: From factories, refineries and power and steel plants release heavy metals such as arsenic, cadmium, copper, chromium, fluoride, mercury, iron, zinc. Hazard: Arsenic causes cancers of the bladder, skin and lung; others weaken teeth and bones weaker, damage vital organs, cause allergies, intestinal lesions.

Food Contaminants: From pesticides, fertilisers, growth hormones, antibiotics such as tetracycline, ciprofloxacin, enrofloxacin and ampicillin given to livestock to prevent disease, accelerate growth and increase feed efficiency. Hazard: Neurotoxin that damages the nervous system, immunity, kidneys, alters genes and causes hormonal imbalances, leading to problems such as early puberty and obesity.

CASE STUDY

Green House Effect

Sankaran Srinivasan, 24, a software engineer with TCS on weekdays, and volunteers with Nalla Keerai (Good Greens), an a group promoting organic farming, over the weekends. He picks up organic produce from a centralised location, takes it to the pre-assigned point for retail distribution, collects money from customers who had already ordered online, and deposits it with Nalla Keerai. He is one of the many college students, software engineers and MNC executives, volunteering with the logistics, marketing and farming of organic produce in the outskirts of Chennai.

The heavily networked brigade is leveraging the social networking sites to build a busy "marketplace". The Facebook page has over 6,000 likes and 2,000 regular customers. They use online order forms to post their requirements, which are sent to farming units. The fresh produce is delivered once a week on Saturdays and grain once a month to 60 different locations, from where volunteers pick up and deliver the produce.

It was Reagannathan who came up with the idea of organic farming. Soon, S. Saravanan, Thirumalai Ranganathan and several others quit the corporate world to take to farming. "Several young people signed up as volunteers because they wanted to do something for the environment, ecology and society". Reanganathan, who met his volunteer wife Anisha while spreading millet over a weekend.

Nalla Keerai, which now deals in 30 varieties of green leafy vegetables and 20 types of millets, has begun to make a difference. Farmers are encouraged to grow more organic varieties as there are no overheads and no middlemen, "Money is directly paid to the farmers, in advance, even before delivery," says Reanganathan.

"We are re-introducing millets as a staple diet, for its health quotient and getting people back to their traditional staple—

Nava Dhanyams. Reanganathan wants to take this model across India, with plans underway to launch Millet Sunday in Bangalore soon. This week, he travelled to Andhra Pradesh to tie up with farmers and share his model with anyone who will see, listen and adopt. Organic produce and traditional staples have to revived, he insists, and he is willing to do the job with a little help from his friends.

Lighting up without Electricity

Arani Chakravarti is a senior professor of Physics, Visva Bharati, but his home at Uttarpalli in Santiniketan has no electricity.

The Chakravarti home has no lights, no fans, no refrigerator, no television not even a motor pump to pump out water. "We don't need those things. We are happy with the way we live, among nature and everything," says Chakravarti, who lives with his wife Samita Seal and sundry strays the couple have adopted.

The couple uses three 12-volt batteries charged using a solar panel to light two small LED bulbs. They have adopted a Roman system for cooling, "We have laid ventilation ducts through a channel of water that cools the air as it enters the room. It brings the indoor temperature down by almost five-degrees, which makes it really comfortable. If we need a breeze, there is hand-fan," smiles Seal.

The Chakravartis and their family—cats, dog, swans, ducks and Cockatiels birds—use only four to five watt of power a day. Handpumps are used to pump water into tanks and reservoir.

It was a stray cat that helped the Chakravartis choose to live like this. "When he joined Visva-Bharati in 1997, we rented a room like everyone else. But then we found an abandoned cat and brought it home, but the neighbours objected, so we decided to have a home of our own," says Seal, who was also a professor of Physics at Suri Vidyasagar College till she resigned in April 2012.

"I recall when we first entered our new home, it was a moonlit night, with natural breeze, something we'd got used to camping for the past one year. We decided that we would continue to live like this," she says. Seal now spends time treating strays using Homeopathy.

"When we moved in, people said you can't go on like this. It's been 13 years and now they appreciate it," says Chakravarti. "It's not easy at first, but once you get started, you love every bit of it," he says.

Water Pollution: Its Impact on Environment and Society
Edited by: Dr. Rabi N. Misra
ISBN: 978-93-5056-790-6
Edition: 2016
Published by: Discovery Publishing House Pvt. Ltd., New Delhi (India)

CHAPTER 8

Pollution of Indian Rivers Effect on Environment

K. Hare Rama Krishna
Lecturer in Commerce, Government College (A), Rajahmundry
(Dr.) Prof. R.N. Misra
Professor in Management Studies, Berhampur, Odisha

Introduction

The Ganges is India's holiest river, considered a source of spiritual purification for devout Hindus. But today the river is among the world's most polluted, struggling under the pressures of modern India.

On the banks of the Ganges River in the Indian city of Varanasi, a man in his thirties is washing clothes by rhythmically hitting on them on a granite slab. Surrounding him on the steps that rise out of the water is a brightly coloured patchwork of saris, drying in the morning sun. The man's name is Vijay Kumar and his family has been working on the river bank washing clothes for generations.

"Every day I'm here," he said. "I start at 5 a.m., then later in the day I iron everything. In the evening I deliver clothes to the customers."

Vijay Kumar's spot on the river is right next to one of Varanasi's traditional cremation areas—a place where Hindus come to burn the bodies of their dead. As he washes clothes, human ashes are dumped into the water just meters away, and smoke from the burning funeral pyres wafts out over the river behind him.

> "It's a problem that the bodies are burning just near to me. But what can I do?" said Vijay. "This is our traditional place to wash clothes, and there is nowhere else to go. The government promised us a new location some years ago, but nothing has changed."

River a Lifeline

Kumar's family has washed clothes for generations

Vijay Kumar is just one of the more than 400 million people who depend on the Ganges River for their livelihoods. But he said he's struggling today because local environmental authorities are trying to shut down his business, saying that his soap suds are polluting the river.

This sort of challenge to balance economic interests and environmental protection is one being played out the world over. But with this river—and particularly here in Varanasi—there is another dimension: the Ganges River is not just an economic lifeline, but also a spiritual one.

Hindus worship the river is as a goddess, Maa Ganga - or Mother Ganga. Anthropologist Dr Assa Doron explained: "The city itself is very much associated with Shiva, and of course Shiva himself has a very strong relationship with the goddess Ganga [...] who has a whole purificatory element - both of them together is what really makes this city shine," he said.

Every year millions of Hindu pilgrims come to Varanasi, seeking spiritual purification in the waters of the Ganges. Many other Hindus who come to Varanasi cremate their loved ones and throw the ashes in the sacred river.

Hindus believe the Ganges to be purifying

Hindus believe that if you die or are cremated in Varanasi, you get moksha—or liberation from the cycles of death and rebirth. But while the river Ganges - known in India as the Ganga - may be pure for religious believers, in secular terms it's in fact gravely polluted.

Multiple River Threats

Varanasi's cremation grounds, however, are just a small fraction of the wider pollution problem facing the Ganges.

Leading water pollution expert B.D. Tripathi of Benares Hindu University described three major Ganges pollution problems: domestic waste, untreated industrial effluent including toxic and heavy metals, and cremation grounds (two in Varanasi alone).

The river runs for some 2,500 kilometers (1,550 miles), with more than two dozen major urban centers located on its banks. With many factories and business dumping toxic chemicals into the river, human sewage compounds the situation.

An estimated 3 billion liters (800,000 gallons) of sewage is released into the Ganges each day, of which only a third - according official figures - is processed by treatment plants. Agricultural businesses are also draining the river basin and adding toxic pesticides and fertilizers into the river system.

Tripathi said that if pollution in the Ganges remains unchecked, the river faces a potentially terminal decline. Without conservation measures, he warned, the river will become fragmented into ponds and streams. "The entire structure of the river will be changed," he said.

Changing and Staying the Same

As India grows economically, those who depend on the river are already bearing witness to the changing health of the river water.

Jaylal Sahani, a boatman now in his 50s, spends his days ferrying pilgrims and tourists in Varanasi. He remembers a time in his childhood when the river was pure enough to drink.

"If we drink the water now, we will get sick," he said.

Kumar, the clothes-washer, says the big factories and businesses are the real problem.

"The government should control the big business and leave us small people in peace. We have no choice but to work here," he said.

Clothes-washers think the main pollution problem is with industry

While modern pollution is forcing many people to break their ties with the river, Hindu scholar Krishnakant Shukla argued that the Ganges's unique place in Hindu cosmology means the river will remain at the heart of Hindu life - however severe the pressures of modern life may become.

Myth lives on in Varanasi, Krishnakant said, "Due to some inexplicable miracle, you can still find people here doing their daily practices the way they did one thousand years ago," he said. "This is amazing - I really don't think there is any other place in the world."

'Untouchable' Indian Scavengers get Social Uplift

A group of low caste 'manual scavengers' have been allowed to take a holy dip in the sacred Ganges River. But will that remove social stigma from the lives of India's untouchables?

Hindus believe a dip where the Ganges, Yamuna and mythical Saraswati rivers meet will cleanse them of their dirt and sins of the past and help them attain salvation. And for the first time, a group of people referred to as "manual scavengers," who are called that because they use wire brushes or shovels and iron pans to clean up and cart away feces from houses that still have bucket or non-flushing toilets, were welcomed by priests to bathe in the Ganges.

Manual scavengers, or toilet cleaners, are viewed as the lowest of the low caste Dalits and are considered to be "untouchables." They are shunned by powerful, high caste Hindus and are not usually allowed to perform such rituals as the Kumbh cleansing dip.

Yet last week, 100 women who used to clean toilets for a living bathed at the site of the Kumbh Mela near Allahabad last week. And afterward, high caste Hindu priests blessed them in ritualistic style, chanting hymns, blowing conchs and smearing them with holy ash.

More than 150 priests and religious leaders, who took part in the ceremony of "Liberation of the Untouchables" as it was called, announced that following the rituals the former manual scavengers were cleansed of all "dirt" of their past. Maharaj Gajanand, a Hindu priest, believes the ceremony marked an important day in Hindu history.

"From today, these sisters will not be considered untouchable in our society," the priest told the media.

Social Uplift

One of the liberated scavengers, Usha Chaumar, looked overwhelmed after the rituals.

India's Kumbh Mela is billed as the world's largest human gathering

"We have been forced to live as outcastes in society. In most cases, we are looked down upon by high caste people who don't socially interact with us," Chaumar, who comes from the Alwar city of the Rajasthan state, told DW.

"I could not believe it when top Hindu priests and community leaders shared meals with us. It felt like I had been reborn."

Chaumar started cleaning bucket toilets of upper caste Hindus when she was a child. But in 2003, she stopped working as a manual scavenger when the social organization Sulabh

International offered her help. The organization developed an eco-friendly and cheap underground toilet systems which convert human waste into fertilizers and bio-fuels. These are known as sulabh toilets in India.

The organization has converted thousands of bucket toilets into sulabh and flush toilets in Alwar and has helped the city's 300 manual scavengers, including Chaumar, find other jobs. Chaumar started an apprenticeship at a Sulabh vocational center and later on became a tailor.

Sulabh International has converted 1.3 million dry toilets and has rehabilitated 1 million manual scavengers across the country in the past four decades, the organization claims.

"By converting bucket toilets and then rehabilitating former scavengers, we help upgrade their economic standard," social activist and founder of Sulabh International Social Service Organization Bindeswar Pathak told DW.

"We helped these people take part in religious rituals at the Kumbh festival. They feel dignified being part of the mainstream now."

'Once a scavenger, always a scavenger'

About 2.6 billion people in India do not have access to toilets and defecate in the open.

However, many believe that the social stigma attached to manual scavengers is too difficult to remove, and that they will not be accepted by the mainstream Hindu society any time soon.

Paras Valmiki, member of the manual scavenger community who works as a peon in a government office in Patna, says that though he has never cleaned toilets, he too is identified as a bhangi, or scavenger, in the society.

"A high caste Hindu peon in my office fell in love with me. But when she learnt that I originally belonged to the scavenger community, she refused to marry me," Valmiki told DW. "It is difficult for us to get rid of the stigma that this society has put upon us."

Jeevan Ram, a railway officer in Hajipur city, is also of the view that taking a holy dip at the Kumbh Mela will not upgrade the societal position of manual scavengers.

"In this heavily caste-based society, it is useless to take some former manual scavengers to temples or help them take dips at Kumbh. When they go back to normal life after these rituals, their social status remains unchanged."

Red water' Muddies Life for Dantewada Villagers

Contamination of water by NMDC iron ore mine's refuse has affected livelihoods

Budhram, a farmer of Kadampal village in Chhattisgarh's Dantewada district, owns five acres of agricultural land and has been monocropping paddy for the past three years. But falling yields have given him cause to worry about the future of his four children.

Paddy production at his farm has fallen by over 50 per cent and Budhram blames this on the contaminated "red water" released from the National Mineral Development Corporation's (NMDC) Bailadila iron ore mine in Kirandul.

"My farm is situated on the banks of the Nala [water stream] and every year during the rains this red water enters my farm and contaminates the fields. Earlier, we used to sow crops twice a year and yet would get good yield. But now even a single-time cultivation is yielding far less than the expected quantity," laments Budhram.

Kadampal is not the only village in Dantewada district affected by the "iron-ore condensed" red water. "Over 55 villages in the district are affected by the iron-ore-particles-mixed water released from the NMDC in Kirandul. Our agriculture land is polluted, our cattle are dying and even drinking water has been affected badly," claimed Raju Karupi of Kadampal.

The affected villagers have formed the Bailadilla Khadan Prabhavit Jan Sangharsh Samiti (BKPJSS) to protest and press for compensation from the NMDC for the damage caused by its pollution.

On May 18, the BKPJSS organised a rally where thousands of affected villagers staged a protest in Kirandul against the NMDC. The BKPJSS has also submitted a 33-point charter of demands to the NMDC and district administration which includes the demand for proper compensation to the farmers affected by red water and the establishment of a water filter plant to curb the release of iron ore particles into the water.

"The NMDC claims to have been doing a lot for the people of Dantewada through its Corporate Social Responsibility (CSR), but it is not even carrying out the basic duties towards the villages it adopted," pointed out Mr. Ramesh Tamu, the secretary of the BKPJSS.

Last year too, villagers submitted complaints and demands, according to Dantewada Collector K.C. Devsenapati.

"A joint team of the district administration, the NMDC and local people conducted a survey of damaged agricultural land and other damages. The NMDC then gave some compensation," the Collector told *The Hindu.*

Mr. Tamu, however, maintains that the compensation was inadequate. "They gave compensation only for the damage done between 2008 and 2012. But people here have been suffering for many years before that. Also, the compensation for the death of cattle was very little," said Mr. Tamu.

Bhima Mandavi, a former BJP MLA from the area, also blamed the NMDC for the red water problem. "The Maoists exploited the water pollution issue in the area. Had the NMDC kept its promises and taken care of the affected villages, Maoists would not have been able to penetrate this area," Mr. Mandavi told *The Hindu.* He had been involved in mobilising villagers against NMDC.

NMDC's Kirandul unit Assistant General Manager Pradeep Saxena refused to comment, saying he was not "authorised" to speak on the issue.

Cleaning Ganga Step by Step

The task of reducing the pollution load of the Ganga is daunting, but the clamour for a cleaner river has gained momentum in recent times.

Traversing over 2,500 km, from the Gangotri glacier in the Himalayas to the Sunderbans delta in Bangladesh, the Ganga is used by hundreds of millions of people. This is one of the few river basins in India that is rich in water resources but highly polluted. How did one of the world's mightiest rivers end up as a garbage dump?

Myriad Issues

Issues affecting the river are myriad and complex. Untreated sewage and industrial waste are dumped into the waters without remorse. Reduced flow and rampant underground water withdrawals affect millions of people who depend on the river's water. Further, floods and droughts, which endanger lives and cause serious damage to crops, livestock and infrastructure, are a common phenomenon in the river basin. A changing climate will pose more challenges. The combination of glacial retreat, decreasing ice mass, early snowmelt and increased winter stream flow will add to the pressure. There is now clear evidence that climate change is already affecting the Himalayan ice cover. This will have a profound impact on the river.

However, all is not lost yet. Recent initiatives by the Indian government such as including 'River Development' and 'Ganga Rejuvenation' to the portfolio of the Minister of Water Resources, and the establishment of the National Ganga River Basin Authority and the National Mission for Clean Ganga, show a commitment to address some of these pressing concerns with special attention given to pollution control.

Even though the task of cleaning the Ganga is a daunting one, significant strides can be made toward achieving this.

Basin-scale Management

The Ganges is a complex transboundary basin which flows across different jurisdictions. Therefore, a basin-scale approach would help manage the water resources better. This would require close coordination with all the countries sharing the Ganga, such as Nepal and Bangladesh, so that the interests of both upstream and downstream users are taken into consideration. The existing treaties on "sharing water resources" could be renegotiated as "shared management of water resources."

Second, the Ganga is highly polluted. Yet, of the 400 million people living along the banks of the river, many still rely on its natural systems for their livelihoods. According to a World Bank report, a number of government efforts (Ganga Action Plan: Phases I and II) have attempted to address the pollution problem, but the results have been disappointing so far. It is estimated that sewage constitutes the largest portion (80 per cent) of the pollution load followed by pollution caused by industrial discharge agricultural activities. With agricultural activities intensifying in areas near the river, particularly in urban and peri-urban areas, fanners frequently rely on wastewater for irrigation. This poses a serious public health risk. However, this adversity can be turned into an opportunity as urban waste offers a significant nutrient resource for farming, if safely treated and applied. Low cost, simple ecological sanitation and reuse systems will be keys to making waste-water treatment feasible for agricultural purposes.

Environmental Flows

Third, environmental flows are essentially the water requirements of aquatic ecosystems and of basic human, social and spiritual needs. However, the concept of environmental flow only refers to the the quantity of water required to maintain river ecology under different environmental conditions. Deteriorating water quality in the Ganga — due to domestic, industrial and agricultural effluents — is also a major threat to riverine ecosystems and to people whose livelihoods depend on water. Innovative methods for maintaining environmental flows and the quality of water during environmentally critical periods, alongwith procedures for implementing these methods, need to be investigated.

In cities, towns and industrial estates most vulnerable to flooding in the Ganges river basin, major investments are required to address climate variability. Existing flood forecasts are often too technical and not easy for the public to understand. Application of remote sensing and hydrological modelling has helped in developing high-quality flood maps, which are useful for developing plans for river conservation, maintaining the quality of water in different stretches and, more importantly, reducing the vulnerabilities of the affected communities.

Innovative approaches such as underground taming of floods for irrigation and aquifer management could offer solutions to the flood problem. These approaches essentially involve storing floodwaters in underground structures in upstream areas. This will help prevent floods and help maintain water availability even during dry seasons.

Toward a Common Goal

In addition to the steps taken by the government to clean the Ganga, successful implementation of this task would require partnerships with various stakeholders. Multiple agencies working to address the problem could be brought on board. The private sector has also shown its willingness to be a partner in cleaning the river, especially at critical points such as Varanasi. Similarly, the public at large, alongwith civil society groups, also need to be actively engaged in these efforts.

In recent times, the clamour for a cleaner Ganga has gained momentum. Although huge progress is being made, the need of the hour is to widen our focus. Negotiations on economic revitalisation of the Ganga should involve India, Nepal and Bangladesh. This task in itself is of mammoth proportions. However, by taking small steps, we can still reduce the pollution load and restore the river to the people.

(Bharat Sharma is principal researcher and coordinator, International Water Management Institute (IWMI), New Delhi. Nitasha Nair, senior communications officer, IWMI, also contributed to this article. The views expressed are personal.)

Restoration of Urban Water Bodies, Berhampur Sets Example for Cities of Odisha

Water bodies are perhaps the only lively Oasis of the Cities. That not only controls temperature but also a source of vegetation. However, many often these oasis are turned into a dumping yards for waste or toilet sheet for informal settlers or unmanaged forestry. Of late cities all over the world are realizing the importance of these water bodies not only for recharging ground water but also into tourist place and more of public space for the citizens by restoring. Similarly it is a source of livelihood for many in urban areas that depend on its products.

Cities are learning the benefits of water bodies within their territory. Same time opportunity of grants from Government is encouraging cities to rejuvenate these water bodies. Berhampur is one such Indian City has restored more than 22 ponds and is in the process of another 17 water bodies. Under UIDSSMT Berhampur city mobilized funds to restore these ponds. Government of India, Government of Odisha and Berhampur Municipal Corporation shares the cost at 80%, 10% & 10% respectively. This is an example of Pro Poor policy.

Berhampur is the fourth largest and one of the oldest cities of India located in southern part of Odisha state. Since 1867 the city is practicing, Municipal Governance. Berhampur is popularly known as Silk City. The city has elected Mayor since 2008. The present population of the city is about 0.35 million with a spread over of 79.80 Sq. km area and 37 wards. Berhampur city is in the process of restoring 270 acres of lands under water bodies.

Situation before the Initiative

The increase in population in the recent decade has transformed lakes and ponds into residential or commercial areas. The disappearance of Berhampur's ponds started in the 80s. Historically there were numerous number ponds existed in this city inter-connected to each other through underground channels. However, over the years these channels were vanished and most of the private owned lakes/ponds were reused for residential and commercial purposes. Meanwhile official statistics today mention existence of 42 lakes / ponds, out of which 39 are in the process of restoration and three are in litigation.

Water bodies in Berhampur are either natural lake, man-made ponds which have been built from the 18th & 19th century to meet the water requirements of the population. Berhampur water bodies are also part of the local hydrologic system. It helps keeping monsoon waters for the drier periods of the year, to canalize these important flows preventing water logging, inundation and erosion, and to ensure the refilling of groundwater. They also support a rich ecosystem, with a great variety of animals and plants. In simple words, water bodies would provide the following:

- Refilling of groundwater, ensuring the bore wells do not dry up.
- Recreational area for the community.
- Regulation of temperature.
- Support a rich ecosystem.

Problems

The water bodies of Berhampur city is in need of a major rejuvenation. Most of these water bodies turned into cesspool and posing health hazard for people living in around and users. These water bodies remained as neglected spots in city maps with no one taking serious actions towards the rejuvenation efforts. As a result:

- The storage capacity got reduced over the years due to silting.
- The weir was damaged and so the water level has gone down.
- The capacity is also reduced. The natural rainwater channels are either blocked or diverted away from the water bodies due to housing construction.
- There is lot of weed and about 80 - 100% water area is covered with weeds.
- The sewerage management was poor and some sewerage flowed into the lake.
- The construction workers and informal settlers at any time in the absence of a proper toilet for them started using these water bodies as a public toilet.

Strategy Adopted

The situation of water bodies has prompted the city council to address the issue and initiate actions. With its limited resources and financial strength, has undertaken this mammoth effort to restore the lake. The criticality of this restoration lies in the fact that:

1. The domestic water needs today are actually met by bore wells in the area. There is a need to ensure that these do NOT GO DRY.
2. There are no other civic amenities or parks in this layout and the ponds is the only lung space.
3. Preservation of the past efforts that have gone into restoring the ponds, thereby ensuring that the efforts do not go in waste.

Innovation

While City Council is debating to restore the water bodies an opportunity was conceived at the Government of India level under the Urban Infrastructure Development Scheme for Small & Medium Towns (UIDSSMT), The Berhampur city approached Government of India for financial assistance to restore these water bodies.

The Berhampur City Council submitted detailed project repot to restore 39 out of 42 water bodies. With basic objectives of improving water quality, recharging of groundwater, provision of water for the animal beings, water for the use of firefighting & construction activity, ensuring aesthetic value of these ponds and use in various cultural activities of human beings. The activities included dewatering, desilting, embankment protection, bathing ghats, pavements, periphery lighting, guard wall, aeration of forty two selected water bodies

Results

The project is approved by Govt. of India with total amount of ₹ 1665.89 Lakhs. In which the share of Government of India would be 80% and 10% each by Government of Odisha (Provincial Government) & Berhampur Municipal Corporation respectively. All these water bodies existing waters were drained in a phased manner and allowing them to dry up in sunlight. Once the water is dried Excavation of earth and silt upto the required depth and removal of silt earth and foreign matters from the container and periphery of the tanks were carried. Then tank bottom surface were filled with granular sand for recharging of ground-water.

The city will restore around 270 acrs of land by the end of pond restoration in 42 water bodies. This is one of the biggest restorations of water bodies practice in urban areas of Odisha.

After restoring the tank beds, bathing ghats around the tanks were also restored or constructed. Similarly the tanks were protected with embankment.

The surrounding areas were landscaped with plants, pavements were constructed for walking, cattle barriers installed, waste bins were placed to protect tanks from Garbage, Lighting arrangement around the tanks to prevent nuisance and messages were placed to build awareness among the people that the tanks are always ready to serve them better. People are using these sites site: for walking, meditation, yoga and leisure. These type of activities were absent previously due to nuisance and misuse of water.

The physical character of water bodies with water quality is improving. The city officials are monitoring the progress of water quality for bathing, drinking by animals and amusement purposes of tourists.

Lessons Learned

Many of our cities environments is actually a gift passed on from our earlier generations. However, many often negligence turns these resources into nuisance. However, today Berhampur city has transformed itself into a responsible institution in managing environmental resources and setting an example for other city in this region.

Sustainability

During the course, city learned more and more about lake/ pond rejuvenation in a holistic sense. That is, to ensure the lake not only is clean, but sustains the test of time. Hence city must keep constant efforts in focusing both aspects of restoration - namely rejuvenation as well as sustenance through regular engagement with citizens and users.

Water Pollution: Its Impact on Environment and Society
Edited by: **Dr. Rabi N. Misra**
ISBN: 978-93-5056-790-6
Edition: **2016**
Published by: **Discovery Publishing House Pvt. Ltd., New Delhi (India)**

CHAPTER 9

Water Pollution and It's Management

Dr. Braja Mohan Sasmal
Retd. Prof. of Chemistry, Sheragada Bunglow, Brahmapur-760 001

Introduction

Water pollution is a major global problem in recent years which requires ongoing evaluation, management and strict implementation of water resource policies for safe survival of plants, animals, aquatic creatures and human being on this earth.

Water pollution is caused by addition of dissolved or suspended solids discharging most dangerous, harmful and toxic pollutants such as detergents, pesticides, heavy metals like Mercury, Lead, Arsenic, Chromium, etc. and non-degradable bio-accumulative compounds, domestic sewages, municipality septic tank and drain water and industrial wastes.

Excess suspended solids present in water will block out energy from the sun and affect the carbon dioxide -oxygen conversion process which is vital to the maintenance of the biological food chain. Also, high concentrations of suspended solids silt up rivers, navigational channels, necessitating frequent dredging. Excess of dissolved chemical liquids and solids make water unsuitable for cooking and drinking purpose and for crop irrigation. The chemicals present in detergents, fertilizer and pesticides on mixing with water, are harmful for survival of aquatic plants and animals. The bacteria present in water will reduce the oxygen content of water and becomes fatal for aquatic plants and animals. Water sources must be prevented from pollution carefully and sterilised by required quantities of bleaching powder and chlorine water to make it free from harmful bacteria. The domestic wastes and industrial wastes should not be mixed with the water sources and these must be sent for recycling and special treatment for purification. Moreover, the chimney emitted acidic gases mixed with rain water in industrial areas must not be added to the water sources during rainy season in order to make water free from different types of pollutants. To prevent water from pollution and contamination, water pollution prevention practices such as low impact development techniques, installation of green roofs and proper management of motor fuels and oils, fertilizers, pesticides, industrial wastes and domestic wastes, run off mitigation systems include infiltration basins, bio-retention systems, constructed wetlands, and other similar devices must be adopted.

Natural phenomenon such as eruption of volcanoes, algae blooms, storms and earthquakes also cause major changes in water quality and the ecological status of water and becomes totally unsuitable for use, by plants, animals and human beings.

Types of Water Pollution

Water pollution may be categorised as (*i*) surface water pollution, (*ii*) Ground water pollution, (*iii*) Microscopic pollution, (*iv*) Thermal pollution, and (*v*) surface pollution.

(*i*) **Surface Water Pollution:** The availability on water surface of earth is possible due to accumulation of rain water in canals, ditches, ponds, rivers, lakes and seas. The surface water can be polluted or contaminated by discharges from canals, sewage treatment plants, factories or city municipal drains due sewer system and liquid wastes from construction sites, cattle farms poultry farms, over fertilised and pesticide fed agricultural fields etc.

(*ii*) **Ground Water Pollution:** The water reservoirs in the underground levels are called as groundwater. By it's very nature, groundwater aquifers are susceptible to contamination from source that may not directly effect surface water bodies. A spill or ongoing releases of chemicals or radionuclide contamination into solid (located away form surface water) may not create pollution, but can contaminate the aquifer below, defined as "toxin plume". Analysis of groundwater contamination may focus on the soil characters and site geology, hydropgeology, hydrology and the, nature of the contaminants present.

(*iii*) **Macroscopic Pollution:** Large sized visible and floatable particles or emulsions fed by urban flood water and marine debris when found on the open rivers and seas cause macroscopic pollution. Such type of water pollution is found to contain the following contaminants as :

Trash or garbages like dust particles, paper pieces, food wastes, plastic sheets discarded by people and thrown on the ground, the rubbish dumped on the ground, and the articles that are washed away by rain water and subsequently discharged into surface water.

(*iv*) **Thermal Pollution:** Thermal pollution is the rise or fall in the temperature of a natural body of water caused by human influence. Thermal pollution unlike chemical pollution results in a change in the physical properties of water. A common cause of thermal pollution is the use of water as a coolant by power plants and industrial manufacturers. Elevated water temperature decreases oxygen levels, which chain composition, can change food reduce species bio-diversity, runoff may also cause such pollution.

(*v*) **Surface Pollution:** Due to leakage of diesels, heavy oils and different petroleum products from the submarines and ships, the water on surface of seas gets polluted. Large quantities of diesels and heavy oils may be discharged on the water surface of seas due to the tilting ships and accident met ships, thereby causing surface pollution of sea water. As a result of this type of pollution, the supply of sunlight and atmospheric oxygen is hindered to greater extent, which may cause causality of aquatic animals like fishes, dolphins, whales etc.

Types of Water Pollutants and Contaminants and their Effects

The specific contaminants leading to pollution in water include a wide spectrum of chemicals and pathogens, which cause physical changes in water, such as elevated temperature and decolourisation. Many of the chemicals and substances are naturally occurring (calcium, sodium, iron, manganese, etc.) high concentration of which can contaminate water. High concentrations of these substances also have harmful impacts on aquatic flora and fauna.

Oxygen depleting substances may be natural materials such as plant materials like leaves and grass as well as man-made chemicals. Other natural and orthopogenic substances may cause turbidity which blocks light and disrupts plant growth, and clogs the gills of some fish and fish like species.

Many of the chemical substances are toxic pathogens can produce water borne diseases in either human or animal hosts. Attention of physical properties of water includes acidity (change of pH), electrical conductivity, temperature and eutrophication, Eutrophication is an increase in the concentration of chemical nutrients in an eco-system to an extent that increases the primary conductivity of the eco-system. Depending on the degree of autrophications, subsequent negative environmental effects such as anoxia (oxygen depletion) and severe reductions in water quality may occur effecting fish and other aquatic animal population:

(*a*) **Pathogens:** Caliform bacteria is commonly used as bacterial eradication of water pollution. Other micro-organisms born tissues found in surface water, which have caused human health problems like Burkholderia pscudomatic cryptosporidium paroicous, salmonella, Giardia Lamblia etc.

High levels of pathogens may result from inadequately treated sewage discharges. This can be caused by a sewage plant designed with less than secondary treatment (more typical in less developed countries) in developed countries older cities with ageing infrastructure may have leaky sewage collection systems (pipes, pumps, valves etc.) which can cause sanitary sewer over lands. Some cities also have combined sewars, which may discharge untreated sewage during rain storms. Pathogens discharges may also be caused by poorly managed livestock operations.

(*b*) **Chemical Contaminants:** Chemical contaminants are of two types namely organic water contaminants and inorganic water contaminants:

(*i*) Organic Contaminants:

(*a*) Detergents.

(*b*) disinfection by products found in chemically disinfected drinking water, such a chloroform or chlorine water.

(*c*) food processing waste, which can include oxygen demanding substances, fats and grease.

(*d*) insecticides and herbicides, a huge range of organohalideds and other chemical compounds.

(*e*) petroleum hydrocarbons, including fuels (gasoline, diesel fuel, jet fuel and stied oils, and lubricants (motor oil), and fuel combustion by products from stream water runoffs.

(*f*) trees and bush debris from logging operations.

(*g*) volatile organic compounds such as industrial solvents from improper storage.

(*h*) Chlorinated solvents, which are dense non-aquous phase liquids, may fall to the bottom of reservoirs, since they do no mix well with water and are denser.

(*i*) Polychlorinated biphenyl.

(*j*) Trichloroethylene.

(*k*) Perchlorate.

(*ii*) Inorganic Water Contaminants

(*a*) Acidity caused by industry discharge (specially sulphur dioxide from power plants).

(*b*) Ammonia from food processing waste.

(*c*) Chemical waste as industrial by products.

(*d*) Fertilizers containing nutrients—nitrates and phosphates which are found in water runoff from agricultural commercial and domestic sources.

(*e*) Heavy metals from motor vehicles and acid-mine drainage.

(*f*) Silt (sediment) in runoff from construction sites, logging, slush and burn particles in land clearing sites.

Adverse Effects of Water Pollutants

Most water pollutants are eventually carried by rivers into the oceans. In some areas of "the world, the influence can be traced hundred miles from the mouth by studies using hydrology transport models. Advanced computer models such as SWMM or DSSAM have been used in n many locations worldwide to examine the fate of pollutants in aquatic systems. Indicator filter feeding species such as copepods have also been used to study pollutant dates in the New York Bright. Fish and shell fish kills have been reported, because toxins climb the food chain after small fishes consume copepods, then larger fishes eat smaller fishes, etc. Each successive step up the food chain causes a stepwise contraction of pollutants such as heavy metals (e.g. mercury) and persistent organic pollutants such as DDT.

Geysers (versters) in the oceans trap floating plastic debris. Many of these long lasting pieces wind-up in the stomach of marine birds and animals. This results in, obstruction of digestive pathways which leads to reduced appetite or even starvation.

Many chemicals undergo reactive decay or chemically change, especially overlong periods of time in groundwater reservoirs. A noteworthy class of such chemicals is the chlorinated hydrocarbons such as trichloroethylene and tetrachloride ethylene used in the cleaning industry. Both of these chemicals which are carcinogens leading to new hazardous chemicals, such as dichloroethylene and vinylchloride.

Groundwater pollution is much more difficult to avoid, than surface pollution because groundwater can move great distances through unseen aquifers. Non-porous aquifers such as clays partially purify water of bacteria by simple filtration (adsorption and absorption), dilution and in some cases the pollutants merely transform the soil contaminants. Groundwater that moves through cracks and caverns is not filtered and can be transported as easily as surface water.

There are a variety of secondary effects stemming not from the original pollutant, but a derivative condition. An example is silt-bearing surface runoff which can inhibit the penetration of sunlight the water column, photosynthesis in aquatic plants.

Measurement of Water Pollution

Water pollution can be analysed through several broad categories of methods: physical, chemical and biological. Most involve collection of samples,' followed- by specialized analytical tests. Some methods may be conducted *in situ,* without sampling, such as temperature. Government agencies and research organizations have published standardized; validated analytical test methods to facilitate the comparability of results from disparate testing events:

(*i*) **Sampling:** Sampling of water for physical or chemical testing can be done by several methods, depending on the accuracy needed and the characteristics of the contaminants. Many contamination events are sharply restricted in time, most commonly in association with rain events. For this reason 'grab' samples are often inadequate for fully quantifying contaminant levels. Scientists gathering this type of data often employ auto-sampler devices that pump increments of water at either time of discharge intervals.

Sampling for biological testing involves collection of plants and/or animals from the surface water body. Depending on the type of assessment, the organism may be identified for bio-surveys and returned to the water body, or they may be dissected for bio-assessment to determine toxicity.

(*ii*) **Physical Testing:** Common physical tests of water include temperature solids concentrations (*e.g.*, total suspended solids (TSS) and turbidity.

(*iii*) **Chemical Testing**: Water samples may be examined using the principles of analytical chemistry. Many published methods are available for both organic and inorganic compounds. Frequently used methods include pH, Biochemcial Oxygen Demand (BOD), Chemical Oxygen Demand (COD), nutrients (nitrate and, phosphorus compounds), metals (including copper, zinc, cadmium, lead and mercury), oil and grease, Total Petroleum Hydrocarbons (TPH) and pesticides.

Management of Control of Pollution

(*i*) **Domestic Sewage**: Domestic sewage is 99.9 per cent pure water, while the other 0.1 per cent are pollutants. Although found in low concentrations, these pollutants pose risk on a large scale. In urban areas, domestic sewage is typically treated by centralized sewage treatment plants. In the U.S., most of these plants are operated by local government agencies, frequently referred to as publicly owned treatment works (POTW). Municipal treatment plants are designed to control conventional pollutants: BOD and suspended solids. Well-designed and operated systems (*i.e.*, secondary treatment or better) can remove 90 per cent or more of these pollutants. Some plants have additional sub-systems to treat nutrient and pathogens. Most municipal plants are not designed to treat toxic pollutants found in industrial wastewater.

Cities with sanitary sewer overflows or combined sewer overflows employ one or more engineering approaches to reduce discharges of untreated sewage, including:

- utilizing a green infrastructure approach to improve storm water management capacity throughout the system, and reduce the hydraulic overloading of the treatment plant.
- repair and replacement of leaking and malfunctioning equipment.
- increasing overall hydraulic capacity of the sewage collection system (often a very expensive option).

A household or business not served by a municipal treatment plant may have an individual septic tank, which treats the wastewater on site and discharges into the soil. Alternatively, domestic wastewater may be sent to a nearby privately owned treatment system (*e.g.*, in a rural community).

(*ii*) Industrial Wastewater: Some industrial facilities generate ordinary domestic sewage that can be treated by. municipal facilities. Industries that generate wastewater with high concentrations of conventional pollutants (*e.g.*, oil and grease), toxic pollutants (*e.g.*, heavy metals, volatile organic compounds) or other non-conventional pollutants such as ammonia, need specialized treatment systems. Some of these facilities can install a pre-treatment system to remove the toxic components, and then send the partially treated wastewater to the municipal system. Industries generating large volumes of wastewater typically operate their own complete on-site treatment systems.

Some industries-have been successful at redesigning their manufacturing processes to reduce or eliminate pollutants, through a process called pollution prevention.

Heated water generated by power plants or manufacturing plants may be controlled with:

- cooling ponds, man-made bodies of water designed for cooling by evaporation, convection and radiation.
- cooling towers, which transfer waste heat to the atmosphere through evaporation and/or heat transfer.
- cogeneration, a process where waste heat is recycled for domestic and/or industrial heating purposes.

(*iii*) Agricultural Wastewater:

(*a*) Non-Point Source Controls: Sediment (loose soil) washed off fields is the largest source of agricultural pollution in the United States. Farmers may utilize erosion controls to reduce runoff flows and retain soil on their fields. Common techniques include contour ploughing, crop mulching, crop rotation, planting perennial crops and installing riparian buffers.

Nutrients (nitrogen and phosphorus) arc typically applied to farmland as commercial fertilizer; animal manure; or spraying of municipal or industrial wastewater (effluent) or sludge. Nutrients may also enter runoff from crop residues, irrigation-water, wildlife and atmospheric deposition. Farmers can develop and implement nutrient management plans to reduce excess application of nutrients.

To minimise pesticide impacts, farmers may use Integrated Pest Management (IPM) techniques (which can include biological pest control) to maintain control over pests, reduce reliance on chemical pesticides and protect water quality.

(*b*) Point Source Wastewater Treatment: Farms with large livestock and poultry operations such as factory farms, are called concentrated animal feeding operations or feedlots in the US are being subjected to increasing government regulation. Animal slurries are usually- treated by containment in anaerobic lagoons before disposal by spray or trickle application to grassland.Constructed wetlands are sometimes used to facilitate treatment animal wastes. Some animal slurries are treated by mixing with straw and composted at high temperature to produce bacteriologically sterile and friable manure for soil improvement.

(*iv*) Construction Site Storm Water: Sediment from construction sites is managed by installation of erosion controls, such as mulching and hydro seeding, Discharge of toxic chemicals such, as motor fuels and concrete washout is prevented by use of:

(*i*) spill prevention and control plans, and

(*ii*) specially designed containers (*e.g.* for concrete washout and structures such as overflow controls and diversion berms).

(*v*) Urban Runoff Stormwater: Effective control of urban runoff involves reducing the velocity and flow of stormwater, as well as reducing pollutant discharges. Local governments use a variety of stormwater management techniques to reduce the effects of urban runoff. These techniques, called best management practices (BMPs) in the U.S., may focus on water quantity control, while others focus on improving water quality and some perform both functions.

CONCLUSION

Water pollution is a major global problem in recent years due to the rapid urbanisation, huge automobile transportations, growing industrialisation and increase of population of the living society. Day by day the original purity of the constituents of air and water of the environment are being poisoned by intermixing of domestic garbages and sewages, industrial wastes (solids, liquids and gases) and automobile exhaust gases.

For safe survival of plants, animals and human beings at present and in future, it requires ongoing evaluation of extent of pollution, management of pollution control and strict implementation of water resource policies and proper storage of pure water for domestic use. Both central and state government authorities should impose strict rules and regulations for adopting present techniques and treatments to control the pollution of water for domestic and industrial purposes and establish Water Pollution Control Boards in every city for timely management of the pollution problems.

Water Pollution: Its Impact on Environment and Society
Edited by: Dr. Rabi N. Misra
ISBN: 978-93-5056-790-6
Edition: 2016
Published by: Discovery Publishing House Pvt. Ltd., New Delhi (India)

CHAPTER 10 Impact of Water Pollution on Health in India —A Study

Prof. G. Chandrayya
Dept. of Commerce, Government College (A), Rajahmundry

(Dr.) Prof. R.K. Misra
Asst. Professor in Management Studies, Bangloor

Introduction

It is a well-known fact that clean water is absolutely essential for healthy living. Adequate supply of fresh and clean drinking water is a basic need for all human beings on the earth, yet it has been observed that millions of people worldwide are deprived of this.

Freshwater resources all over the world are threatened not only by over exploitation and poor management but also by ecological degradation. The main source of freshwater pollution can be attributed to discharge of untreated waste, dumping of industrial effluent, and run-off from agricultural fields. Industrial growth, urbanization and the increasing use of synthetic organic substances have serious and adverse impacts on freshwater bodies. It is a generally accepted fact that the developed countries suffer from problems of chemical discharge into the water sources mainly *groundwater*, while developing countries face problems of agricultural run-off in water sources. Polluted water like *chemicals in drinking water* causes problem to health and leads to. *water-borne* diseases which can be prevented by taking measures can be taken even at the household level.

Groundwater and its Contamination

Many areas of groundwater and surface water are now contaminated with heavy metals, POPs (persistent organic pollutants), and nutrients that have an adverse affect on health. Water-borne diseases and water-caused health problems are mostly due to inadequate and incompetent management of water resources. Safe water for all can only be assured when access, sustainability, and equity can be guaranteed. Access can be defined as the number of people who are guaranteed safe drinking water and sufficient quantities of it. There has to be an effort to sustain it, and there has to be a fair and equal distribution of water to all segments of the society. Urban areas generally have a higher coverage of safe water than the rural areas. Even within an area there is variation: areas that can pay for the services have access to safe water whereas areas that cannot pay for the services have to make do with water from hand pumps and other sources.

In the urban areas water gets contaminated in many different ways, some of the most common reasons being leaky water pipe joints in areas where the water pipe and sewage line pass close together. Sometimes the water gets polluted at source due to various reasons and mainly due to inflow of sewage into the source.

Groundwater can be contaminated through various sources and some of these are mentioned below:

Pesticides: Run-off from farms, backyards, and golf courses contain pesticides such as DOT that in turn contaminate the water. Leechate from landfill sites is another major contaminating source. Its effects on the ecosystems and health are endocrine and reproductive damage in wildlife. Groundwater is susceptible to contamination, as pesticides are mobile in the soil. It is a matter of concern as these chemicals are persistent in the soil and water.

Sewage: Untreated or inadequately treated municipal sewage is a major source of groundwater and surface water pollution in the developing countries. The organic material that is discharged with municipal waste into the watercourses uses substantial oxygen for biological degradation thereby upsetting the ecological-balance of rivers and lakes. Sewage also carries microbial pathogens that are the cause of the spread of disease.

Nutrients: Domestic wastewater, agricultural run-off, and industrial effluents contain phosphorus and nitrogen, fertilizer run-off, manure from livestock operations, which increase the level of nutrients in water bodies and can cause eutrophication in the lakes and rivers and continue on to the coastal areas. The nitrates come mainly from the fertilizer that is added to the fields. Excessive use of fertilizers cause nitrate contamination of groundwater, with the result that nitrate levels in drinking water is far above the safety levels recommended. Good agricultural practices can help in reducing the amount of nitrates in the soil and thereby lower its content in the water.

Synthetic Organics: Many of the 100,000 synthetic compounds in use today are found in the aquatic environment and accumulate in the food chain. POPs or Persistent Organic Pollutants, represent the most harmful element for the ecosystem and for human health, for example, industrial chemicals and agricultural pesticides. These chemicals can accumulate in fish and cause serious damage to human health. Where pesticides are used on a large-scale, groundwater gets contaminated and this leads to the chemical contamination of drinking water.

Acidification: Acidification of surface water, mainly lakes and reservoirs, is one of the major environmental impacts of transport over long distance of air pollutants such as sulphur dioxide from power plants, other heavy industry such as steel plants, and motor vehicles. This problem is more severe in the US and in parts of Europe.

Chemicals in Drinking Water

Chemicals in water can be both naturally occurring or introduced by human interference and can have serious health effects.

Fluoride: Fluoride in the water is essential for protection against dental caries and weakening of the bones, but higher levels can have an adverse effect on health. In India, high fluoride content is found naturally in the waters in Rajasthan.

Arsenic: Arsenic occurs naturally or is possibly aggrevated by over powering aquifers and by phosphorus from fertilizers. High concentrations of arsenic in water can have an adverse effect on health.A few years back, high concentrations of this element was found in drinking water in six districts in West Bengal. A majority of people in the area was found suffering from arsenic skin lesions. It was felt that arsenic contamination in the groundwater was due to natural causes. The government is trying to provide an alternative drinking water source and a method through which the arsenic content from water can be removed.

Lead: Pipes, fittings, solder, and the service connections of some household plumbing systems contain lead that contaminates the drinking water source.

Recreational use of Water: Untreated sewage, industrial effluents, and agricultural waste are often discharged into the water bodies such as the lakes, coastal areas and rivers endangering their use for recreational purposes such as swimming and canoeing.

Petrochemicals: Petrochemicals contaminate the groundwater from underground petroleum storage tanks.

Other Heavy Metals: These contaminants come from mining waste and tailings, landfills, or hazardous waste dumps.

Chlorinated Solvents: Metal and plastic effluents, fabric cleaning, electronic and aircraft manufacturing are often discharged and contaminate groundwater.

Disease

Water-borne diseases are infectious diseases spread primarily through contaminated water. Though these diseases are spread either directly or through flies or filth, water is the chief medium for spread of these diseases and hence they are termed as water-borne diseases:

Cause	Water-borne diseases
Bacterial infections	Typhoid Cholera Paratyphoid fever, Bacillary dysentery
Viral infections	Infectious Hepatitis (jaundice) Poliomyelitis
Protozoal infections	Amoebic dysentery

Most intenstinal (enteric) diseases are infectious and are trnasmitted through faecal waste. Photogens—which include virus, bacteria, protozoa, and parasitic worms—are disease-producing agents found in the faeces of infected persons. These diseases are more prevalent in areas with poor sanitary conditions. These pathogens travel through water sources and interfuses directly through persons handling food and water. Since these diseases are highly infectious, extreme care and hygiene should be maintained by people looking after an infected patient. Hepatitis, cholera, dysentery, and typhoid are the more common water-borne diseases that affect large populations in the tropical regions.

A large number of chemicals that either exist naturally in the land or are added due to human activity dissolve in the water, thereby contaminating it and leading to various diseases.

Pesticides: The organophosphates and the carbonates present in pesticides affect and damage the nervous system and can cause cancer. Some of the pesticides contain carcinogens that exceed recommended levels. They contain chlorides that cause reproductive and endocrinal damage.

Lead: Lead is hazardous to health as it accumulates in the body and affects the central nervous system. Children and pregnant women are most at risk.

Fluoride: Excess fluorides can cause yellowing of the teeth and damage to the spinal cord and other crippling diseases.

Nitrates: Drinking water that gets contaminated with nitrates can prove fatal especially to infants that drink formula milk as it restricts the amount of oxygen that reaches the brain causing the 'blue baby' syndrome. It is also linked to digestive tract cancers. It causes algae to bloom resulting in eutrophication in surface water.

Petrochemicals: Benzene and other petrochemicals can cause cancer even at low exposure levels.

Chlorinated Solvents: These are linked to reproduction disorders and to some cancers.

Arsenic: Arsenic poisoning through water can cause liver and nervous system damage, vascular diseases and also skin cancer.

Other Heavy Metals: Heavy metals cause damage to the nervous system and the kidney, and other metabolic disruptions.

Salts: It makes the fresh water unusable for drinking and irrigation purposes.

Exposure to polluted water can cause diarrhoea, skin irritation, respiratory problems, and other diseases, depending on the pollutant that is in the water body. Stagnant water and other untreated water provide a habitat for the mosquito and a host of other parasites and insects that cause a large number of diseases especially in the tropical regions. Among these, malaria is undoubtedly the most widely distributed and causes most damage to human health.

Preventive Measures

Water-borne epidemics and health hazards in the aquatic environment are mainly due to improper management of water resources. Proper management of water resources has become the need of the hour as this would ultimately lead to a cleaner and healthier environment.

In order to prevent the spread of water-borne infectious diseases, people should take adequate precautions. The city water supply should be properly checked and necessary steps taken to disinfect it. Water pipes should be regularly checked for leaks and cracks. At home, the water should be boiled, filtered, or other methods and necessary steps taken to ensure that it is free from infection.

Minamata: Environmental Contamination with Methyl mercury

In Minamata, Japan, inorganic mercury was used in the industrial production of acetaldehyde. It was discharged into the nearby bay as wastewater and was ingested by organisms in the bottom sediments. Fish and other creatures in the sea were soon contaminated and eventually residents of this area who consumed the fish suffered from MeHg (methyl mercury) intoxication, later known as the Minamata disease. The disease was first detected in 1956 but the mercury emissions continued until 1968. But even after the emission of mercury stopped, the bottom sediment of the polluted water contained high levels of this mercury.

Various measures were taken to deal with this disease. Environmental pollution control, which included cessation of the mercury process; industrial effluent control, environmental restoration of the bay; and restrictions on the intake of fish from the bay. This apart research and investigative activities were promoted assiduously, and compensation and help was offered by the Japanese Government to all those affected by the disease.

The Minamata disease proved a turning point, towards progress in environment protection measures. This experience clearly showed that health and environment considerations must be integrated into the process of economic and industrial development from an early stage.

The Effects: Human Health

Nutrient pollution and harmful algae blooms create toxins and compounds that are dangerous for your health. There are several ways that people (and pets) can be exposed to these compounds.

Direct Exposure to Toxic Algae

Drinking water can be a source of exposure to chemicals caused by nutrient pollution.

Drinking, accidentally swallowing or swimming in water affected by a harmful algae bloom can cause serious health problems including:

- Rashes.
- Stomach or liver illness.
- Respiratory problems.
- Neurological affects.

Nitrates in Drinking Water

Nitrate, a compound found in fertilizer, often contaminates drinking water in agricultural areas. Infants who drink water too high in nitrates can become seriously ill and even die. Symptoms include shortness of breath and blue-tinted skin, a condition known as blue baby syndrome.

A 2010 report on nutrients in ground and surface water by the U.S. Geological Survey found that nitrates were too high in 64 per cent of shallow monitoring wells in agricultural and urban areas.

Byproducts of Water Treatment

Stormwater run-off carries nutrients directly into rivers, lakes and reservors which serve as sources of drinking water for many people. When disinfectants used to treat drinking water react with toxic algae, harmful chemicals called dioxins can be created. These byproducts have been linked to reproductive and developmental health risks and even cancer.

Sources and Causes of Water Pollution

The causes of water pollution is directly related to the type of water pollution in question. Pollutants may be natural or human caused, and may include contaminants that can affect water quality such as nutrients, sediments, organochlorines, heavy metals, oil and hydrocarbons, chemical constituents and pathogens.

1. **Eutrophication:** This is when a water body has a lot of pollutants containing nutrients thrown into it in a way that increases algae and plant growth in the water. This hurts animal life in that water because soon, the massive growth of algae consumes all the oxygen in the water, starving other animal life. Eutrophication is caused by

increased application of fertilizers, waste from animal and households, as well as land clearing for agricultural purposes. Eutrophication is common in estuaries, but with recent increase in global temperatures, there is a threat that the effect will be felt in the oceans to which the estuaries are connected.

2. **Microbial Pollution:** This results from poor treatment of human sewage as well as poor treatment of sewage from large or industrial farms such as those found in Upper Uruguay. The pathogens in microbial pollution are a major health hazard, especially in areas with poor drinking water treatment.
3. **Solid Waste:** Poor waste disposal activities is probably the culprit here. Visit beaches and water recreational joints to witness all sorts of rubbish piles washed ashore by the water. This is not only a horrible sight, but also cause harm to humans and animals as well. The trans-boundary effect of this makes it worse, as the rubbish can be transported thousands of miles from one place to the other. *In addition to locally produced solid waste, an estimated 700,000 tonnes of solid waste is generated annually by the 35 million tourists who visit the Caribbean, many on cruise liners.*
4. **Chemical Pollution:** Agricultural run-off, municipal waste discharges, mining and industrial discharges, landfills and atmospheric transport add up to a massive occurrence of chemicals being discharged into water bodies. Persistent organic pollutants such as furans and dioxins, as well as heavy metals like mercury and cadmium can be transported over long distances when dissolved in water. Large scale pesticides applied to sugarcane on plantations in Central America have had negative effects on the health of people there and is believed to have resulted in reduced fish stocks in the Nicoya Gulf of Costa Rica.
5. **Oil Pollution:** Oil drilling, refining and transportation have long been a major issue especially with marine

pollution. We depend so much on oil that it is hard to put in place very tough controls to prevent it. Oil spills form tankers and vessels cause a lot of short and long term harm to water life. *Nearly 5000 oil spills in the Niger River delta were reported between 1976 and 1996, releasing nearly 375,000 tonnes of oil in total. This has resulted in groundwater contamination and a loss of biodiversity in the vicinity of oil installations.* In recent time, there has been some genuine concern about 'Tracking' as a process of shale gas extraction

Preventing Water Pollution

It is easy to be overwhelmed by the problem of water pollution and think that individuals cannot make a difference. If each person in a township can be responsible in the way they deal with waste, sewage and the things that cause pollution, there would be a remarkable improvement to the problem. Preventing water pollution can be a two way approach.

Individuals

1. Know where all your drains and sewage lead to and make an effort not to throw wastewater into drains. If there are

organic matter in your waste or sewage, think of ways to compost them, or follow laiddown instructions given by your local council on how to dispose off organic waste.

2. Ensure that you comply with the waste disposal arrangements made by your council.
3. Reduce waste creation. We all have a rather bad culture of want and waste. It is possible for each family or individual to reduce consumption and waste by half. The less we consume of everything, the less would be produced by manufacturing industries and farms. Ultimately resulting in less pollution.
4. Look out for, and be mindful of where to dispose off hazardous chemicals and medicines. Your local council or police station can assist with information on how to dispose off chemicals and hazardous waste.

Policy

Government policies and laws can make a world of difference. Here is what can be done:

1. Governments can invest in research, and assist with the provision of logistics for industries, farms and businesses to dispose off waste. Planning with these industries and farms creates an awareness of the consequences of their actions and establishes a commitment to reducing the negative impact of nutrient pollution.
2. Education on the dangers of water pollution is extremely important, as it helps people to apply the right attitudes when dealing with the environment. Education activities that get people informed and empowered to help protect water should be encouraged and invested in.
3. Laws must be enforced, with very hefty fines and actions for industries that do not comply with water pollution prevention laws. If industries know that they are being monitored and checked regularly, they will usually ensure best practices of waste and chemical dumping at all cost.

Water Pollution: Its Impact on Environment and Society
Edited by: **Dr. Rabi N. Misra**
ISBN: 978-93-5056-790-6
Edition: **2016**
Published by: **Discovery Publishing House Pvt. Ltd., New Delhi (India)**

Polluted Bahana Canal
The 'Sorrow' of Brahmapur

Dr. Bharatha Panda
Ph.D., M.A., B.Ed., L.L.B., Former Principal Parsuram Gurukula Mahavidyalaya, Sevakpur, Orisha

Introduction

The eightfold divisions of Nature (Earth, Water, Fire, Air, Ether, Mind, Reason/and Egoism) constitute the inferior nature, (apara prakriti) It constitutes the Khetra or the field or matter. It is impure. The superior nature is pure. These two natures, the inferior and the superior, are the womb of all beings. The Blessed Lord said: O Arjuna! This body is called the Field (Khetra); he who knows the field is known as the knower of the field (Khetrajna), the wise who know the both declare so. Thus, this body is vehicle is the Kshetra and the pure intelligence is the knower of the field. The manifestations of the Lord is described in Bhagavad Geeta, that is the Lord is the rapidity in water. So to say the water is life and the Vayu is Prana. In short it can be said the body is to be compared to a short world, belongs to Pancha tatwa along with mind, reason and egoism, include in Prakriti and grosser elements. In short it is declared by God that Purusha is the matter and cause of all creations, sustenance and destruction of the entire universe. Prakriti is the instrument with which he creates, maintains and destroys the whole universe. Hence the Lord declared His Omnipresence in four Vedas. That is—

"Raso' hamapsu Kauntey prabha' smi Sasisurya yah,

Pranavah sarva vedasu sabda khe Prauraham Nrishu"

Thus the Lord explains that He is the taste in the watertight in the Sun and the Moon, Oum in the Vedas, sound in Ether and virility in men. Hence it is clear that the ruling pincilple is the flora and fauna cannot survive without life. Thus the flora and fauna on earth are formed with the five elements but the infra of the body water. Hence, the water is the life and air is the prana, one can live without food days together but cannot live without water. For the existence of life water plays a unique role in all the biological process. The pure water, fresh water creates fresh status in mind and polluted water causes a lot of diseases. Water is a precious gift of God. That is why we worship Varuna and Indra, who are the in charge of supply of water in the world. During Puja we offer pure water to God. Dysentery, Typhoid, fever. Goiter, parasitic diseases, round worm, guinea worm are caused by drinking impure water. Swamy Sivananda Saraswati says that use of impure and polluted water leads to general lower state of health and increased susceptibility to diseases. Impure air and impure water, infected food, uncleanness of houses and its surroundings, improper and bad disposal of excretion play a vital part in the dissemination of disease. It is observed by the scientists that 0.007 per cent of water is available for the human consumption on earth out of the total water available on earth. 2,500 years ago a leading professor in Taxasila indicated the infrastructure of a village:

"Sotriya, Banika, Raja nadi Vaidtashu Panchahamam,

Pancha jahara nabaratnant tasmas vasa Nakerayat."

That is, Sotriya means the Priest, Vanika—the businessman, Praja—the King, Nadi or river, vaidya, the doctor are the five subjects are necessary to establish a village, otherwise the place is not suitable for residence, to get pure water the river is the main source for flora and fauna for existence of life. Let us see the causes of pollution of water in the world. Scientific report says "since 1900 the world's population has more than tripled to six billion, according to UN. The 14 hottest years since the records began in 1866 have occurred up to 1980. The world's average surface temperature has risen by up to one degree centigrade bringing the threat of melting ice caps and rising sea level. Environmentalists say that the problem of fresh water supply is likely to be most important issue of 21st century. According to world wild life statistics about one-fifth of equatorial forest were lost between the year 1960 and 1990. As a result of that about 31,000 plant and animals species face the threat of extinction. The ozone layer, which envelops the earth as a protective cover was discovered in 1985. It is caution to mankind. It is observed that one-sixth of world's population do not have access to safe drinking water. To acquire sound heath pure drinking water is required.

Sources of Water

There are six sources of water in the world, they are:

- Seventy per cent of water covered on earth.
- Total quantity of water – 32.2 crores cubic miles.
- Usable water 0.3 per cent,
- Per cent of salty water in the oceans – 99.7.
- About 0.3 per cent water is below the ground level,
- The total reserved water is 32.6 cubic miles of which 300 cubic miles are used practically which is 1/1000 per cent.

Table 1: Source of Water in the World

Source	Quantity of Water Lakh Cubic Miles	Per cent
Oceanic Water	3170.00	97.24
Iceland Glaciar Water	70.00	2.14
Under Groundwater	20.00	0.61

Source	Quantity of Water Lakh Cubic Miles	Per cent
Sweet Water (Lake)	0.30	*
Sea on Earth Water	0.25	*
Earth Wet Water	0.16	*
Earth Water	0.03	*
River Water	0.003	*
	3260.743	99.99

Serial No. 4 to 8 equals to 0.01 per cent.

Source: Annual Journal, Orissa Environmental Society, 2004.

The beasts have no knowledge on pollution of water but man is intelligent. We can control the pollution. The causes of above water be minutely observed to find out the solution to control the pollution.

Earlier it is discussed that water is indispensable for the maintenance of life, both for animals and vegetables. Pure water is very beneficial to health like pure air and pure food. Pure water consists of oxygen 88.89 per cent and Hydrogen 11.11 per cent. The chemical formula is H_2O. Rain water is the purest water. Springs are natural wells; fit for drinking. Spring water is pure. Wells are three kinds: (1) Shallow wells-Polluted water, (2) Deep wells-tube wells, (3) Artesian wells-used for cultivation of land. A good well should satisfy the following conditions: good soil, 200 meters from trenching ground distance, 100 meters from human habitation. Good construction and every year it should be cleaned and maintained. Upland water, tanks, ponds, reservoirs, rivers and streams are surface water which must be purified. Purification of water can be done through sun light, air, oxidization and settlement and artificial methods, *i.e.* (1) Physical (distillation and boiling), (2) Chemical (precipitation and germicides), and (3) filtration (slow sand filters and rapid filters) through filtration all superficial matters are removed.

Pollution in Brahmapur City

In towns and cities alongwith the citizens it is the duty of the City Corporation and municipalities to keep the town clean and supply pure drinking water to the people. From geography we learn that the river Hoyang Ho is the sorrow of China. River Kathjodi and Mahanadi of Odisha are described as sorrow of Cuttack and Rushikulya is the sorrow of Aska; Vanshadhara is the sorrow of Kasinagar and the Bahana canal is the sorrow of Brahmapur corporation, with reference to sanitation, drainage system, sanitary system and control of flood.

First of all the historical background of historical place of Brahmapur has to be discussed. Then only the glory of the past will come to light. Mr. T.J. Meltby a British Officer at Madras in 19th century gives a vivid account of Brahmapur city. This is the main source to know the details of Ganjam district and Brahmapur town in the past. The population of the city was 21, a86 in 1871. Brahmapur was a municipality having residence of civil and sessions Judge of Ganjam. The old Brahmapur is exclusively the native part of the town. Even though there are no rivers nearby Brahmapur, there are numerous small tanks and irrigation canals, swollen during monsoon rains. Since the establishment of the municipality in 1867, the health of the town is steadily improving but much have to be done to improve the sanitary condition.

Bahana Pollution

Efforts have been made earlier in nineteenth century to solve the water problem of the district, for the purpose cultivation and drinking purposes. The two projects were:

(1) **Chilka Canal:** A canal to connect Chilka lake and Kalingapattam is an old scheme approved by Col. Cotton long bake. It was taken as famine work in 1865 and completed up to river Rushikulya at Ganjam town and also up to Gopalpur but could not reach up to Kalingapattam due to insufficient funds.

(2) The Janibil-Rushikulya Project (1891) supplies water to Brahmapur town through Bahana Nalla which carries polluted water of Brahmapur and flows up to Bay of Bengal.

Brahmapur city is now widely extended which can be geographically located as five "G's City, as it starts from Girisula in the south-west and ends at Ganjam town on the banks of Rushikulya. I feel that the Bahana canal which flows in the middle of Brahmapur city can be termed as Sorrow of Brahmapur for the following reasons:

1. Bahana Nala carries the polluted water of the city and no arrangements are made for its maintenance, the result of which it become the breeding centre of mosquitoes and produced different spots in the town area.
2. The bridges over Bahana Nala of new Brahmapur are smaller than the old bridges. Hence the heavy rainy water overflows the embarking.
3. The culverts of the connected canal occupied by the people and houses are constructed.
4. In the learned and literate area no drainage system rules are followed.
5. The houses are constructed encroaching the drains and the drains are being narrowed.
6. The water level went to unreachable ground level due to the coverage of old tanks for apartment purposes.
7. Stagnant polluted water is seen in the Bahana Nala throughout the year and in the rainy season it floods to the quarters by the side.

CONCLUSION

The Bahana Canal which is described as "The Sorrow of Brahmapur" can be restored to its former condition, instead of spreading diseases to the citizens of the city it can provide pure water and healthy atmosphere to the people in the area through which it flows, If sincere efforts are made, by the people and the Corporate Administration, it is possible.

We suggest these measures for its rehabilitation which would help the citizens of the town to live a healthy life:

1. The position of Bahana Nala prior to the construction of buildings and apartments be recovered and the polluted water to the Bay of Bengal.
2. The canal road be constructed in such a height that it can be helpful to the people to save their life during heavy rains and terrible flood site and the road be used for communication purpose.
3. The streets should be constructed with strong cement roads, which will give scope to vacate the water as the streets are converted into canals.
4. During the summer season scanty of water is run as the irrigated tanks are covered, the result of which water level reached un-reachable ground level and the wells are dry.
5. The last slogan is a request to the intellectuals to save the city and save the deserted world.

Index

J

K

L

M

N

O

P

R

S

T